Ickworth Parish Registers: Baptisms, Marriages And Burials, 1566 To 1890

Sydenham Henry Augustus Hervey

Ickworth, Eng. (Parish)

ICKWORTH
PARISH REGISTERS.

Baptisms, Marriages & Burials.

1566 TO 1890.

Wells:
ERNEST JACKSON, 5, HIGH STREET.
1894.

CONTENTS.

CORRIGENDA ET NOTANDA.

P. 4, l. 2.—Probably this name is Stuttevile.

P. 11, l. 5.—No year is given, so it is impossible to say whether this entry belongs to 1700 or 1701.

P. 16.—Between 1808 and 1811 no years are given, and I found it impossible to fix them. It must not be supposed that all these belong to 1808.

P. 69.—"Except Nos. 31 and 32" should be "except Nos. 32 and 33."

In Baptisms, Sept. 1832, Sep. 1837, Oct. 1843, Sept. 1845, Nov. 1846, for Lady Katherine Hervey read Lady Katherine Jermyn.

ILLUSTRATIONS.

PREFACE.

IT is to be hoped that before very long every Parish in the land will be compelled by law to have its Registers printed. It should be done at the expence of the rates, unless the Parish chooses to do it otherwise. But it should be done somehow, and that right soon. That there should be these valuable and interesting documents lying unprinted, and therefore unsecured against destruction, is simply disgraceful. To print is to preserve. Who prints, preserves ; who says, Don't print, practically says, Don't preserve, or at any rate Don't secure, which is nearly as bad. But besides preserving and securing, printing also unlocks the chest, and sends the knowledge of its contents to whosover will have it. And surely there must be some in all quarters of the world, who desire to know the contents of the parish chest, when that parish has been the home and the sepulchre of their fathers.

The Parish Registers of Ickworth are in good preservation. They begin in 1566, and from that year to this there is no gap. Even the Civil War of the 17th Century does not seem to have disturbed the even tenor of their course. There are signs of carelessness in the very early years of this century, and again during the Incumbency of the Rev. Dr. Burgess between 1870 and 1880 ; and of course at any time single entries may have been occasionally omitted ; but in spite of such actualities and possibilities the Registers are a remarkably complete record for over 300 years.

The number of entries during the 325 years is as follows : Baptisms, 725 ; Marriages, 250 ; Burials, 520. Many of the marriages in the 17th and 18th centuries were of people who had nothing to do with Ickworth, and why they came there I don't know. It is plain that with an average of 2 Baptisms and 1½ Burial in a year, we have not got to deal with a population of thousands, nor even of hundreds. An interesting survey of Ickworth made in 1665 has lately been printed, which gives the number of acres in Ickworth belonging to the owner of the Hall as 1188, divided (excepting 76 acres of wood) amongst 18 farms. If the houses of those 18 farms were all in Ickworth, as they appear to have been, then they with cottages and other tenements that there probably were would bring the population up to between 100 and 200. But since John,

Lord Bristol, made Ickworth his home in 1702, and gradually removed the village and restored and enlarged the park, the population, I expect, has seldom reached 100. (See Census Returns, at the end of this Volume, p. 92.)

Of houses which might have seen the men of the 16th and 17th Centuries, scarcely one remains. Ickworth Lodge and perhaps the present Dairy may have done so, but no other. The original Hall, just outside the Churchyard wall, is clean gone. A dry summer shows where its foundations are, and the kitchen garden would not be where it is if the old Hall had not been where it was; except for that, there is no vestige of it above ground. The old Parsonage also is clean gone. (See page 83-87 of this vol.) The Parson's pond remains to show where it was, but that is all. The village is gone; the 18 farm houses are gone. Ickworth Lodge may represent one of them, and the Dairy may represent another; but the others have left nothing behind, not even a memory; had it not been for the Survey of 1665, one would never have so much as dreamed of their existence. The blacksmith's shop was on the site of the present Mordeboys Cottages, conveniently situated by the side of the then high road from Bury to Chevington. There Benjamin Summers shod horses whilst the first two Georges were on the throne, and I don't know how many of his fathers had done so before him.

With regard to the illustrations, the 5 heraldic shields printed separately with the letter-press are copied from the Visitation of Suffolk. I have elsewhere expressed my thanks to Mr. J. J. Howard for his permission to do so. After they had been printed I found amongst some papers belonging to my father drawings of all the shields (except one) in Ickworth Church. These drawings had been made by the Rev.— Francis, formerly curate of Great Saxham. I therefore had them engraved on two plates, of course leaving out the five which I had already copied from the Visitation of Suffolk. The one shield which Mr. Francis had not drawn was that of John, Lord Hervey, whose stone is under the pulpit and quite unreachable. However, I am able to include that also, as Mrs. George H. W. Hervey has been good enough to reach the unreachable, and make a rubbing of it. At the same time Mrs. Hervey was able to set at rest a doubtful point as to the date of birth of Lady Hervey. Gage (History of Thingoe Hundred) had made the inscription say that she was born Sept. 26, 1706; Mr. J. J. Howard (Visitation of Suffolk) and others had repeated this; but as she was a Maid of Honour in 1717, and married in 1720, it was obviously impossible. It now turns out that the inscription (correctly copied by Sir John Cullum) gives the year of her birth as 1700, and not 1706; so that "the uncertainty" (Dict. of Nat. Biog :) was only the result of Mr. Gage's error.

I have elsewhere expressed my thanks to Mr. Gery Milner-Gibson-Cullum for sending me a transcript of Sir John Cullum's Notes on Ickworth, which I have printed at pp. 79-82.

I should like to have added the notes made by Henry Chitting, Chester Herald, soon after 1600, and those made by Francis Blomefield about 1720, both quoted by Gage (Thingoe Hundred), but I have not been able to find them out.

There only remains for me to express my best thanks to the Rev. James Giddens, Rector of Ickworth, first for allowing me to transcribe and print these Registers, and secondly for his kindness in revising the proofs by the original volumes.

S. H. A. H.

Wedmore Vicarage,
June 1894.

ICKWORTH PARISH REGISTERS.

BAPTISMS.

1566.	June	25.	Ambrose sonne of William Hervey, Esqre.
	March	9.	John sonne of John Oylett.
	March	13.	Arthur sonne of Robert Spalding.
1567.	April	25.	Rose daughter of Henry Mayhew.
	Feb.	16.	John sonne of John Oylett.
	Sept.	23.	Robert sonne of Richard Paman.
1568.	July	31.	Bridget dau: of William Hervey Esqre.
	March	12.	Robert sonne of Henry Mayhew.
1570.	Nov.	27.	Robert sonne of William Hervey, Esqre.
1571.	Nov.	18.	John sonne of John Barret.
	Nov.	19.	Juliane daughter of Jane Oylett.
	Jan.	13.	Mary daughter of Henry Mayhew.
1572.	July	13.	Elizabeth daughter of William Lynge.
1573	June	28.	ffrances daughter of John Oylett.
	Aug.	2.	William sonne of John Barret.
1574.	Jan.	23.	Audry daughter of William Lynge.
	July	4.	Georg sonne of Austin Pamman.
1575.	Dec.	18.	Agnes daughter of Thomas Johnson.
	Jan.	15.	Catherine daughter of Edward Barret.
1576.	April	29.	Robert sonne of John Barret.
	April	29.	Anne daughter of James Lardiner.
	Dec.	23.	Mary daughter of William Lynge.
1577.	Aug.	11.	John sonne of Edward Barret.
1578.	Aug.	24.	ffrances daughter of Edward Barret.
	Oct.	5.	Isebella daughter of William Lynge.

1578. Oct.   26. Thomas sonne of Thomas Sarpar.
1579, April   5. James sonne of James Lardiner.
      April   26. Elizabeth daughter of John Barret.
1580. May   11. ———— daughter of John Oylett.
      May   18. Francis sonne of John Barret.
1581. July   4. Francis sonne of John Barnes.
      Nov.   5. John sonne of John Adams.
1582. July   22. ———— daughter of Thomas Wadilow.
1583. Dec.   1. Ralf sonne of John Adams.
      Dec.   15. John sonne of Edward Heldersom.
      Jan.   1. Bridget daughter of John Barret.
      Jan.   19. Jone daughter of Thomas Johnson.·
      March   8. Anne daughter of John Mud.
1584. Aug.   1. Agnes daughter of Thomas Wadilow.
      Jan.   1. John sonne of John Dowsyng.
1585. April   12. Richard sonne of Francis Ling.
      March   20. Frances daughter of Thomas Wadilow,
1586. April   25. Alyse daughter of John Barret.
      Oct.   9. Anne daughter of Peter Doddle.
1587. April   17. Amy daughter of Robert Adams.
      May   8. Samuel sonne of Samuel Colle.
      Aug.   18. ffrancis sonne of Edward Hildersom.
      Jan.   7. Sarah daughter of Thomas Russel.
1588. March   27. Susan daughter of John Hervey, Gent,
      April   13. Marke sonne of John Barret.
      July   14. Agnes daughter of Thomas Maye.
      March   15. John sonne of John Hervey, Gent.
1589. May   11. Edward sonne of ffrancis Ling.
      June   1. Margaret daughter of John Mud.
      June   24. John sonne of Robert Newgate.
      Aug.   3. Elizabeth daughter of John Dowsen.
      Sept.   7. Elizabeth daughter of Robert ffortune.
      Nov.   20. Mary daughter of John Hervey, Gent.

1592.	Feb.	20.	Jane daughter of John Barret.
	May	28.	—— sonne of Robert ffortune.
	Aug.	6.	Eve daughter of —— Goodday.
	Nov.	4.	John sonne of James Manning.
1593.	March	4.	Thomas sonne of John Dowsing.
1594.	May	12.	Margaret daughter of John Mudd.
	Oct.	17.	Edmund sonne of John Hervey Esqre.
	Oct.	20.	Mary daughter of Steven Tany.
	Nov.	3.	Margaret daughter of Robert ffortune.
1595.	Oct.	29.	Robert sonne of John Hervey Esqre.
	Feb.	22.	Elizabeth daughter of William Ellett.
1596.	April	4.	John sonne of William Briand.
1597.	Dec.	4.	John sonne of William Elliot.
	Jan.	22.	Robert sonne of William Briant.
	Feb.	12.	ffrances daughter of John Hervey Esqre.
	March	12.	Abigal daughter of Richard Castrick.
1598.	May	14.	John sonne of Edward Wakefeild.
	Aug.	6.	Eustraus sonne of Peter Diggle.
1599.	June	24.	William sonne of William Ellett.
	July	8.	Dorothe daughter of Elizabeth Poley.
	Sept.	29.	Susan daughter of William Withers.
	Oct.	14.	Margaret daughter of Oliffer Steel.
1600.	Nov.	9.	Liddia daughter of —— Cestrick.
	Dec.	14.	Adrie daughter of —— Elliott.
1601.	Oct.	4.	William sonne of William Withers.
	Nov.	14.	Thomas sonne of Oliffer Steel.
	Feb.	17.	Mary daughter of John Parker.
	Feb.	20.	Elizabeth daughter of Thomas Payten.
1602.	Aug.	2.	Rose daughter of Peter Diggle.
1603.	April	17.	Anne daughter of Thomas Payten.
	Jan.	29.	George sonne of Ollifer Steel,
1604.	May	15.	Anne daughter of Arthur Gutterich.
	May	17.	Elizabeth daughter of William Withers.

1604.	July	29.	John sonne of John Buckenham.
1605.	Aug.	21.	Thomas sonne of Thomas Stutteinle (or Stuttenile ?)
	Jan.	19.	Rose daughter of William Ellett.
	Jan.	19.	Isabell daughter of Thomas Payten.
1606.	April	8.	Edward sonne of William Withers.
	April	13.	Henry ⎫ sons of John Buckenham. Ambrose ⎭
	April	13.	Mary daughter of Oliffer Steel.
	April	15.	Elizabeth daughter of Arthur Gutterich.
	May	4.	William sonne of Richard Castrick.
1607.	March	28.	Elizabeth daughter of Elizabeth Poley.
	Jan.	17.	John sonne of John Buckenham.
1608.	Feb.	2.	Anne daughter of Arthur Cutterice.
1609.	July	16.	Mary daughter of Thomas Payton.
	Sept.	20.	John sonne of William Withers.
	Jan.	28.	Mary daughter of John Buckenham.
			Richard sonne of Abraham Person.
1610.	Aug.	12.	Mary daughter of John Waterhouse.
	Sept.	2.	Mary daughter of John Smith.
1611.	March	31.	John sonne of John Harison.
	Oct.	13.	James sonne of William Withers.
	Nov.	6.	Mary daughter of Arthur Cutterice.
	Dec.	5.	Joane daughter of John Buckenham.
	Feb.	2.	Margaret daughter of William Boyden.
1612.	May	1.	John sonne of John Waterhouse.
	May	10.	Susan daughter of John Ballard.
	June	2.	Philippe daughter of Abraham Person.
	July	25.	John sonne of John Cheston.
	Sept.	10.	Elizabeth daughter of Thomas Payton.
1613.	May	20.	Thomas sonne of William Withers.
	Dec.	28.	Thomas sonne of John Waterhouse.
1614.	April	14.	Elizabeth daughter of Arthur Cutterice.
	July	14.	Samuel sonne of Samuel Martin Esqre.

1614.	Sept.	25	Thomas sonne of Thomas Bray.
	Oct.	30.	Sarah daughter ot Thomas Ruggles.
	Nov.	27.	William sonne of William Boytene.
	Jan.	8.	Thomas sonne of Thomas Paytone.
	March	2.	Mary daughter of Robert Cole.
1615.	Sept.	19.	John sonne of Samuell Martin, Esqre.
1616.	Aug.	27.	John Hervey the sonne and heire of Sir William Hervey, Knight.
1617.	April	13.	William sonne of Richard Ware.
	June	8.	Edward sonne of Henry Spencer.
	June	8.	Elizabeth daughter of Henry Myles.
	Sept.	21.	Susanna daughter of Thomas Paytone.
1618.	July	5.	Martha daughter of John Ballard.
	Aug.	9.	Edward sonne of John Baylie.
	Nov.	1.	Gabrell sonne of William Lyng.
	Nov.	22.	William sonne of John Waterhouse.
	Dec.	6.	John sonne of William Boytene.
	Feb.	24.	Elizabeth daughter of Richard Ware.
1620.	May	31.	Mary daughter of Sir William Hervey.
	Aug.	20.	Rachell daughter of Henry Myles.
	Oct.	29.	Susanna daughter of John Waterhouse.
	Dec.	10.	Francis sonne of John Ballard.
	Jan.	28.	Charles sonne of William Boytene.
1621.	April	2.	John sonne of John Bayly.
	July	23.	Susan daughter of Sir William Hervey.
	Jan.	13.	Frances daughter of Richard Ware.
1622.	April	14.	Elizabeth daughter of Robert Crysol.
	May	8.	Thomas sonne of John Firmine.
1623.	July	4.	Anne daughter of John Waterhouse.
1624.	June	20.	Anne daughter of Thomas Nunne.
	June	27.	Henry sonne of Richard Ware.
	July	25.	Robert sonne of Robert Hammant.
	Dec.	12.	Henry sonne of Henry Miles.

1624.	Feb.	28.	Mary daughter of John Firmine.
1625.	July	29.	Audry daughter of Thomas Nunne.
	Jan.	8.	Robert sonne of John Waterhouse.
1626.	Oct.	25.	Margaret daughter of Thomas Nunne.
	Nov.	26.	Martha daughter of Robert Hammant.
	Jan.	11.	Hasset sonne of Francis Wells.
	Feb.	25.	Mary daughter of Edward Gippes.
1627.	Sept.	23.	Elizabeth daughter of John Firmin.
	Nov.	18.	Susan daughter of Henry Miles.
1628.	June	6.	Martha daughter of Raynold Whayman.
1629.	April	25.	William sonne of Robert Hammant.
	June	16.	John sonne of John Beale, Clerk.
	March	9.	William sonne of William Johnson.
1630.	April	4.	Clement sonne of John Firmin.
	Aug.	17.	John sonne of Robert Hammond.
1631.	Nov.	3.	Henry sonne of William Johnson.
	Dec.	28.	Mary daughter of William Sudbury, Clerk.
1632.	April	12.	John sonne of Peter Cooke.
	March	21.	John sonne of Richard Spencer.
1633.	June	20.	Margaret daughter of Robert Hammond.
1634.	April	20.	Anne base child of Anne Jakes.
	May	27.	Elias sonne of William Johnson.
	Nov.	12.	Daniell sonne of William Sudbury.
1635.	April	22.	Anne daughter of Richard Spencer.
	June	17.	Mary daughter of Robert Hammond.
	Aug.	13.	Elizabeth daughter of Thomas Mayhew.
1636.	March	30.	John sonne of John Waterhouse.
1637.	July	2.	Prudence daughter of Richard Dawkins.
	Oct.	28.	Susan daughter of William Sudbury.
	Oct.	29.	Thomas sonne of Thomas Mayhew.
1639.	March	29.	Sarah daughter of John Summers.
	Sept.	15.	Elizabeth daughter of John Waterhouse.
	Nov.	20.	Anne daughter of John Dearesley.

1639.	Jan.	25.	Elizabeth daughter of William fford.
	March	17.	Elizabeth daughter of John Summers.
1640.	Feb.	3.	Samuell sonne of William Sudbury.
1641.	April	27.	Mary daughter of William fford.
	Nov.	18.	Susan daughter of John Dearesly.
1643.	Jan.	28.	Margaret daughter of William fford.
1645.	April	17.	Mary daughter of William fford.
	May	27.	Mary daughter of John Summers.
	Nov.	16.	Thomas sonne of Mary Waterhouse.
1647.	Oct.	23.	Bridget daughter of John Summers.
	Dec.	30.	Mary daughter of Robert Bilham.
1648.	Dec.	9.	Mary daughter of Arthur Goodchild.
	Jan.	9.	John sonne of John Loker, Cler :
	Feb.	8.	William sonne of John Ellis.
1649.	Feb.	14.	Robert sonne of Robert Bilham.
1650.	Aug.	17.	John sonne of John Summers.
	Nov.	25.	Margaret daughter of John Loker, Cler :
1651.	April	28.	Dorothie daughter of John Heward.
	Feb.	2.	Thomas sonne of John Mayhu.
1652.	June	26.	Susan daughter of Arthur Goodchild.
	July	9.	Susan daughter of Thomas Furmin.
	Aug.	26.	Margaret daughter of Francis Evat.
	Aug.	31.	Susan daughter of John Loker, Cler :
1653.	July	22.	John sonne of Thomas Furmin.
	Sept.	13.	Martha daughter of John Summers.
	March	2.	Robert sonne of John Goodale.
1654.	May	11.	ffrances daughter of Arthur Goodchild.
	June	22.	John sonne of John Mayhu.
	Sept.	7.	Frances daughter of Robert Heward.
	Dec.	28.	Francis sonne of Francis Evat.
	Jan.	1.	Mary daughter of John Loker, Cler :
1655.	April	9.	Elizabeth daughter of Thomas Furmin.
	June	22.	Francis sonne of Arthur Goodchild.

1655.	Aug.	2.	Sarah daughter of Edward Godfrey.
1656.	May	3.	Thomasin daughter of Thomas Furmin.
	May	26.	Thomas sonne of Thomas Merton.
	Aug.	29.	James sonne of John Loker, Cler :
	Aug.	31.	Margaret daughter of John Mayhu.
	Nov.	25.	Arthur sonne of Arthur Goodchild.
	Feb.	17.	Henry sonne of Francis Evat.
1657.	Nov.	26.	Elizabeth daughter of Edward Godfrey.
	Feb.	20.	Thomas sonne of Francis Evat.
1658.	Nov.	1.	Eleanor daughter of John Loker, Cler 1
1659.	March	29.	John sonne of Thomas Merton.
	March	29.	Rachel daughter of Thomas Merton.
	Aug.	7.	Thomas sonne of John Mayhu.
1660.			Henry sonne of Edward Baythorne.
	May	29.	Thomas sonne of Thomas Mayhu.
	Aug.	16.	Anne daughter of Francis Evat.
	Jan.	13.	Robert sonne of John Loker.
1661.	May	19.	John sonne of Edward Godfrey.
	Aug.	4.	Thomas sonne of Thomas Merton.
	Dec.	12.	Joseph sonne of John Mayhu.
1663.	May.	17.	Richard sonne of Richard Ward.
	Feb.	11.	Mary daughter of Thomas Smith.
	March	6.	Isabell daughter of Edward Godfrey.
	March	13.	Mary daughter of Francis Evat.
1664.	Feb.	23.	Richard sonne of Edward Baythorne.
1665.	July	7.	Agnes daughter of Francis Evat.
	Jan.	11.	Mary daughter of Thomas Smith.
1666.	Jan.	10.	Thomas sonne of Edward Baythorne.
	Jan.	20.	Elizabeth daughter of Francis Evat.
1668.	May	1.	John sonne of John Chapman.
	May	22.	Penelope daughter of Edward Baythorne.
	July	5.	Thomas sonne of Edward Godfrey.
	July	23.	Luke sonne of John Mayhu.

1669.	Aug.	29.	Agnes daughter of Francis Evat.
	Nov.	7.	John sonne of John Turner.
	Feb.	15.	William sonne of Edward Baythorne.
1670.	May	29.	William sonne of John Mayhu.
	March	7.	Elizabeth daughter of John Turner.
1671.	March	3.	Frances daughter of Francis Evat.
1673.	July	6.	John sonne of John Summers.
	Sept.	12.	Robert sonne of Robert Feild.
	Nov.	14.	Elizabeth daughter of John Wyard.
1675.	May	25.	Margaret daughter of John Turner.
	May	30.	Elizabeth daughter of John Summers.
1677.	May	17.	Mary daughter of Arthur Goodchild.
	Sept.	6.	John sonne of Thomas Nun.
	Jan.	8.	Mary daughter of Robert ffield.
1678.	Jan.	9.	Jeremiah sonne of John Adams.
	Jan.	31.	Thomas sonne of Thomas Nun.
1679.	Nov.	11.	George sonne of James Weyard.
1680.	June	24.	Lidea daughter of John Adams.
	Dec.	10.	Frances daughter of Thomas Nun.
1681.	Sept.	26.	Charles sonne of (blank)
1682.	June	26.	Benjamin sonne of John Summers.
	Dec.	28.	Thomas sonne of Arthur Goodchild.
1683.	April	26.	Elizabeth daughter of James & Elizabeth Weyard.
	Aug.	26.	Thomas sonne of Thomas & Abigal Murton.
1584.	Sept.	26.	James sonne of Thomas & ffrances Nun.
	Nov.	21.	William sonne of William & Elizabeth Hempstead.
1685.	Aug.	8.	Edward sonne of Edward & Susan Goodchild.
	Aug.	11.	George sonne of James & Elizabeth Wyard.
	Jan.	10.	William sonne of Thomas & Abigal Murton.
	Feb.	14.	Sarah daughter of John & Abigal Heward.
1686.	Aug.	24.	Arthur sonne of Arthur & Sarah Goodchild.
	Aug.	26.	Elizabeth daughter of William & Elizabeth Hempsted.
	Feb.	17.	Abigal daughter of John & Abigal Heward.

B

1687. April 29. Alice daughter of Edward & Alice Goodchild.

Dec. 27. Hannah daughter of James & Elizabeth Wyard.

1688. Sept. 6. Abraham sonne of Thomas & ffrances Nun.

Sept. 9. Samuel sonne of Samuel & Susan Norman.

Sept. 22. Mercy sonne (sic) of John & Abigal Heward.

Nov. 8. Abigal daughter of Thomas & Abigal Murton.

Feb. 24. Sarah daughter of Robert & Anne Mitchen.

1689. June 6. Elizabeth daughter of Edward & Alice Goodchild.

Aug. 1. Mary daughter of Antony & Katerine Hollax.

March 14. Margaret daughter of James & Elizabeth Wyard.

1690. May 29. Elizabeth daughter of Thomas & ffrances Nun.

Jan. 15. ffrances daughter of John & Abigal Heward.

Jan. 27. John sonne of Thomas & Abigal Murton.

Feb. 22. Alice daughter of James & Elizabeth Wyard.

1691. April 19. Mary daughter of Robert & Anne Mitchen.

Oct. 9. John sonne of Edward & Alice Goodchild.

1692. Jan. 9. Alice daughter of John and Alice Frost.

1693. July 20. Joseph son of Joseph & Frances Alexander was baptized in Horninsheth, and was received into ye congregation July 30 following.

Sept. 28. Frances daughter of James & Elizabeth Wyard.

Nov. 7. Hugh son of Hugh & Alice Spencer.

Dec. 5. Mary daughter of Thomas & Abigal Murton.

1694. Nov. 18. John son of Joseph & Frances Alexander.

1695. April 5. Thomas son of Edward & Alice Goodchild.

July 13. Elizabeth daughter of John & Alice Frost.

Sept. 6. Alice daughter of Hugh & Alice Spencer.

Dec. 6. Frances daughter of Joseph & Frances Alexander.

1696. June 18. Rebecca daughter of Thomas & Christian Ling.

1697. Sept. 16. Frances daughter of Joseph & Frances Alexander.

Oct. 1. John son of Hugh and Alice Spencer.

Nov. 28. Thomas son of Thomas & Christian Ling.

1698. Oct. 28. Mary daughter of Joseph & Frances Alexander.

1699. May 28. William son of Hugh & Alice Spencer.

July 14. John son of Hugh & Elizabeth Pattle.

Oct. 14. Mary daughter of John & Alice Frost.

Dec. 16. John son of Thomas & Christian Ling.

Jan. 18. Judith daughter of Joseph & Frances Alexander, being born Thursday Jan. 4.

1701. Aug. 7. William son of Joseph & Frances Alexander, being born July 28.

Jan. 30. James son of Thomas & Christian Ling.

Feb. 5. Elizabeth daughter of Hugh & Alice Spencer.

1702. Sept. 18. Marget daughter of Joseph & Frances Alexander was born at Horninsheth Sept. 9, 1702, and baptized in the said town of Horninsheth Sept. 18.

1703. Aug. 30. Elizabeth daughter of Richard & Elizabeth Everard.

Oct. 11. Lucy daughter of Thomas & Christian Ling.

1704. Oct. 19. Thomas son of Hugh & Alice Spencer.

1705. March 16. Robert son of Richard & Elizabeth Everard.

1706. May 12. Samuel son } of Thomas & Christian Ling.
Mary daughter }

1707. Sept. 25. Paul son of Hugh and Alice Spencer.

Oct. 5. Ann daughter of Richard & Elizabeth Everard.

Oct. 31. Sarah daughter of Joseph & Frances Alexander.

1708. June 3. Humphry son to ye Right Honourable John Lord Hervey Baron of Ickworth, and ye Right Honourable Lady Elizabeth his wife.

Oct. 12. Elizabeth daughter of Thomas & Christian Ling.

1709. Sept. 23. Elizabeth daughter of Thomas & Christian Ling.

Feb. 20. Benjamin son of Richard & Elizabeth Everard.

1710. March 8. Ralph son of Hugh & Alice Spencer.

1711. May 10. Francis son of Joseph & Frances Alexander.

Feb. 19. James son of Thomas and Christian Ling.

1712. May 25. Susan daughter of Richard & Elizabeth Everard.

1713. Aug. 13. Sarah daughter of Benjamin & Sarah Summer.

1713.	Feb.	11.	Mary base child of Rebecca Ling.
1714.	Oct.	18.	William son of William & Mary Larner.
	Oct.	25.	James son of Richard & Elizabeth Everard.
1715.	Jan.	8.	Arthur son of Arthur & Marget Goodchild.
1716.	June	7.	John son of Benjamin & Sarah Summer.
1717.	Nov.	24.	Thomas son of William & Mary Larner.
	Jan.	12.	Frances daughter of Thomas & Frances Ling.
1719.	Feb.	7.	John son of Thomas & Frances Ling.
1721.	March	21.	Thomas son of John & Mary Everett.
	April	7.	John son of John & Mary Everett.
1722.	Sept.	30.	Mary daughter of Thomas & Frances Ling.
	Nov.	26.	John son of John & Mary Everet.
1724.	July	17.	Benjaman son of Benjaman & Sarah Summer.
	Jan.	18.	Henary son of Henary & Sary Everet.
1725.	Aug.	16.	Mary dafter of John & Mary Everet.
	Jan.	17.	Rebacke dafter of Henry & Sary Everet.
1727.	April	29.	Mary dafter of Robert & Rose Stocking.
	June	11.	Thomas son of Thomas & Frances Ling.
	Feb.	21.	Francis son of John & Mary Everard.
1728.	March	8.	William son of Thomas & Elizabeth Nun.
	Feb.	25.	William son of Henary & Sarah Everard.
1729.	Sept.	21.	Diane daughter of William & Suzan Emet.
1730.	Feb.	11.	Samawall son of John & Mary Evered.
1732.	Aug.	4.	William son of William & Suzan Emet.
	Aug.	20.	Mary daughter of Henry & Sary Everet.
1733.	May	20.	Mary daughter of Robert & Rose Stocking.
1734.	April	7.	Thomas son of John and Mary Everrad.
1738.	Aug.	25.	Elizabeth daughter of John & Mary Everett.
1739.	April	23.	Elizabeth daughter of Joseph & Susanna Prick.
1740.	March	22.	Philip son of James & Rose Crick.
1741.	April	24.	Joseph son of Joseph & Susanna Prick.
1743.	May	29.	Philip son of James & Rose Crick.
	Feb.	9.	Susanna daughter of Joseph & Susanna Prick.

1745. Oct. 31. John son of James & Rose Crick.
1746. Nov. 15. Mary daughter of Joseph & Susanna Prick.
1747. Jan. 17. William base born son of Elizabeth Lilly.
1748. March 24. William son of James & Rose Crick.
Sept. 7. George William, the son of Constantine Phipps Esq., was publicly baptized at Ickworth; privately baptized at Horringer, Aug. 6.
1748/9 Feb. 25. Elizabeth daughter of Joseph & Susanna Prick.
1749. April 9. Charles John Castalio, a negroe.
Oct. 20. Sarah daughter of James & Rose Crick.
1750/1 March 3. Elizabeth base born daughter of Diana Boyle.
1752. Aug. 9. Grace daughter of James & Rose Crick.
Oct. 22. Mary daughter of William & Mary Fenton.
1754. May 18. William son of William & Mary Fenton.
1755. Oct. 3. Anne daughter of James & Rose Crick.
1758. March 19. George son of William & Mary Emmet.
Nov. 10. Anne daughter of Robert & Elizabeth Bridges.
1760. Feb. 28. Robert son of Robert & Elizabeth Bridges.
Aug. 3. Rose daughter of John & Rose Everett.
1761. March 8. Theophilus son of Robert & Elizabeth Bridges.
May 14. Sarah daughter of ——— & Sarah Frost.
1762. Jan. 10. Ann daughter of William & Mary Emmet.
Jan. 10. Thomas son of Thomas & ——— Everett.
March 21. ——— of Robert & Elizabeth Bridges.
1763. April 3. Rose daughter of Robert & Martha Stocking.
May 1. Ann daughter of William & Mary Emmet.
1764. April 15. Robert son of Robert & Martha Stocking.
April 29. Anne daughter of William & Mary Emmet.
Nov. 11. Elizabeth daughter of Joseph & ——— Prick.
1765. April 7. John son of Robert & Martha Stocking.
1767. April 12. Susanna daughter of William & Mary Emmet.
1768. Oct. 23. Elizabeth daughter of Thomas & Sarah Everett.
1769. Feb. 18. James son of Robert & Martha Stocking.

1772.	May	24.	Rose daughter of Robert & Martha Stocking.
	July	22.	John son of Mary Tilson.
	Nov.	15.	John son of William & Mary Emmett.
1774.	Feb.	6.	Lydia daughter of Joseph & Elizabeth Prick jun.
1775.	Nov.	26.	Mary daughter of John & Mary Winch.
1776.	Sept.	1.	Sarah daughter of Joseph & Elizabeth Prick.
1777.	April	27.	Elizabeth daughter of John & Mary Wynch.
1780.	Sept.	4.	Elizabeth Catherine Caroline daughter of John Lord Hervey & Lady Hervey.
	Dec.	16.	Augustus John William son of —— & Lady Elizabeth Foster.
1781.	Dec.	30.	Robert son of Robert & Martha Stockin.
1782.	April	8.	Hannah daughter of James & Hannah Button.
	May	12.	John son of John & Elizabeth Alvis.
	May	12.	Alice daughter of Joseph & Elizabeth Prick.
1783.*	May	10.	Mary daughter of James & Hannah Button.
1784.	March	14.	Sarah daughter of John & Ann Green.
	Oct.	29.	Augustus son of Thomas & Elizabeth Aves (late Prick).
	Nov.	21.	Charlotte Kemp daughter of Ann Crick.
1785.	Feb.	7.	Benjamin son of Benjamin & Mary Prick (late Lumley).
	May	15.	John son of John & Mary Moore (late Towers).
	Dec.	4.	Susan daughter of Rose Prick.
1786.	June	21.	John son of James & Hannah Butten (late Petit).
	Dec.	24.	Elizabeth daughter of John & Elizabeth Green.
1787.	Oct.	7.	William son of Thomas & Elizabeth Aves.
	Nov.	27.	James son of James & Hannah Button.
	Dec.	27.	Henry son of Benjamin & Mary Prick.
1789.	July	26.	Hannah daughter of James & Hannah Button.
1790.	Oct.	17.	Sophy daughter of Benjamin & Mary Prick (late Lumley).

* This and nearly every succeeding Baptism for the next 20 years is entered as Private. These infants could not all have been in a precarious state, so I presume that they were privately baptized in accordance with the custom of the day or of the place. The date of reception into the Church is also given; but I have not thought it worth while to print that. The mother's maiden name is also given in brackets. S.H.A.H.

1791.	July	31.	Thomas son of Thomas & Mabel Evered (late Steed).
1792.	March	18.	Stephen son of John & Mary Winch (late Sharpe).
1793.	July	14.	Harriot daughter of Benjamin & Mary Prick.
1794.	Jan.	12.	Abraham son of Thomas & Mabel Evered (late Steed).
	Aug.	10.	John son of John & Mary Winch.
1796.	Jan.	10.	John son of William & Dorothy Richardson.
	March	8.	Maria Frances, daughter of Rev. Joseph Sandys & Frances his wife, late of Kilrea in the Kingdom of Ireland, was born and baptized the same day.
	May	29.	Lucy daughter of Benjamin & Mary Prick.
1797.	March	8.	Frederic son of Thomas & Mabel Evered (late Steed).
	April	9.	Robert Winch.
	April	9.	Ann Green received into the Church at 16 years of age.
	July	16.	William Robert son of the Rev. Joseph Sandys & Frances his wife (late Burroughs) of Kilrea in the Kingdom of Ireland. Born July 4.
1799.	Oct.	20.	Elizabeth daughter of John & Ann Winch (late Sharpe).
	Oct.	30.	Anthony Thomas son of Benjamin & Mary Prick (late Lumley).
1801.	Jan.	18.	Mabel daughter of Thomas & Mabel Evered (late Steed).
1802.	Jan.	31.	Mary daughter of John & Ann Winch (late Sharpe), received into the Church.
	Nov.	26.	Stephen son of John & Ann Gossick (late Curtis).
	June	20.	Hannah daughter of James & Sarah Bullis (late Avis).
	Nov.	21.	Elizabeth daughter of William & Susannah Syer (late Prick).
1803.	Aug.	14.	John son of John & Ann Gossick (late Curtis).
1804.	April	8.	Eliza daughter of William & Elizabeth Jennison (late Roots).
	May	20.	Suzan daughter of John & Ann Winch (late Sharpe).
1805.	May	13.	John son of John & Ann Lennard (late Green).
	Feb.	25.	Sophia daughter of John & Mary Hammond (late Stocking).

1805. Sept. 30. Maria daughter of Robert & Alice Copsey (late Pearson).

Sept. 15. Thomas son of John & Ann Gossick (late Curtis).

Dec. 21. Born, Maria daughter of William & Elizabeth Jennison (late Roots).

1806. May 29. William son of William & Mary Emmett (late Hempsted.)

Nov. 7. Fanny daughter of John & Ann Winch (late Sharpe).

* Oct. 12. Joseph son of Robert & Mary Avis (late Parfory).

March 4. Maria daughter of James & Lydia Howe (late Wells).

Sept. ·21. Received into the Church Mary & Sarah daughters of William & Sarah Green (late Briant).

Feb. 3. Thomas son of Thomas & Ann Lennard (late Green).

1808. Jan. 31. Elizabeth daughter of William & Elizabeth Jennison (late Roots).

June 21. James son of Abraham & Mary Albon (late White).

Aug. 9. Frank son of John & Ann Gossick (late Curtis).

Aug. 23. John son of John & Mary Hammond (late Stocking).

Feb. 7. Jane daughter of William & Sarah Seal (late Richardson) ·, Born July 7.

Feb. 7. Thomas son of Frances Green. Born July 9.

Dec. 21. John son of John & Susan Osborne (late Holden,.

Feb. 9. Robert son of Robert & Mary Avis (late Parforey).

April 24. Phyllis daughter of Thomas & Ann Leonard (late Green).

Aug. 3. George son of William & Sarah Green (late Bryant).

Dec. 25. Susan dau: of John & Ann Winch (late Sharpe). Born July 31.

Aug. 13. Ann daughter of Abraham & Mary Albon (late White). Born July 30.

Sept. 3. Mary daughter of John & Ann Gossick (late Curtis). Born July 13.

---

* Some of the ensuing dates are dates of Birth, some of Baptism, some of reception into the Church. Often for the next five years no year is given, so I have not put one in.   S.H.A.H.

June 4. Henry son of James & Lydia Howe (late Wells). Born Dec. 11, 1808.

March 23. Marianne daughter of John & Mary Hammond (late Stocking). Born Feb. 5.

June 3. Harriot daughter of William & Elizabeth Jennison (late Roots).

June 22. Born & Baptized William son of Robert & Sarah Rolfe (late Farrance).

1811. Sept. 1. Sarah daughter of John & Ann Winch (late Sharpe).

July 1. William son of William & Sarah Sale (late Richardson). Born May 28.

Feb. 2. Shadrach son of James & Mary Cross (late Wallis). Born Jan. 5.

Feb. 9. William son of Abraham & Mary Albon (late White). Born Jan. 1.

Feb. 15. Rose daughter of Joseph & Sarah Pryke (late Cooper.)

Feb. 17. David son of John & Mary Hammond (late Stocking).

July 27. Marianne daughter of Robert & Sarah Rolfe (late Farrance).

1812. June 7. Mary daughter of Edmund & Mary Willingham (late Brewster).

Aug. 13. Jane daughter of William & Elizabeth Jennison (late Roots).

Sept. 20. John son of John & Mary Finch (late Cobbing).

1813. March 28. Maria daughter of William & Sarah Sale (late Richardson) of Ickworth, Labourer.

March 28. John son of Mary Lanham of Ickworth, servant.

June 27. Thomas Frederic son of James & Lydia Howe (late Wells) of Chevington, Farmer.

Aug. 8. George Farrance son of Robert & Sarah Rolfe (late Farrance) of Ickworth, Gamekeeper.

1814. Jan. 9. Sarah daughter of Frances Green of Ickworth.

C

1814. April 17. David son of Thomas & Ann Lennard (late Green), of Ickworth, Labourer.

May 22. John son of James & Mary Cross (late Green) of Ickworth, Labourer.

March 27. Mary daughter of William & Elizabeth Jennison (late Roots) of Ickworth, Gardiner.

May 29. David and Robert sons of John & Mary Hammond (late Stocking) of Ickworth, Labourer.

July 31. Elizabeth daughter of Abraham & Mary Albon (late White) of Ickworth, Labourer.

Nov. 13. Thomas son of John & Mary Finch (late Cobbing).

1815. *March 20. George son of John & Elizabeth Cator (late Edwards), of Ickworth, Labourer.

Sept. 9. Mary Anne daughter of William & Ann Anderson (late Burton) of Ickworth, Gardiner.

Nov. 7. Joseph } sons of Robert and Sarah Rolfe (late Farrance) & William } of Ickworth, Keeper.

1816. May 19. Ann daughter of Thomas & Ann Lennard (late Green) of Ickworth, Labourer.

June 23. Mary daughter of James & Mary Cross (late Wallace) of Ickworth, Labourer.

June 30. Sarah daughter of William & Sarah Sale (late Richardson) of Ickworth, Labourer.

July 28. Jane daughter of Abraham & Mary Albon (late White) of Ickworth, Labourer,

Aug. 4. Martha daughter of John & Mary Hammond (late Stocking) of Ickworth, Labourer.

1817. Aug. 13. Eliza daughter of John & Mary Finch (late Cobbing) of Ickworth, Groom.

1818. Jan. 25. Jemima daughter of James & Mary Cross (late Wallace) of Ickworth, Labourer.

---

* This entry is made five years late, viz., in 1820.—S. H. A. H.

1818. March 15. Sarah daughter of Robert & Sarah Rolfe (late Farrance) of Ickworth, Keeper.

April 5. Thomas son of Abraham & Mary Albon (late White) of Ickworth, Labourer.

Aug. 18. William son of Thomas & Susan Ely (late Manning) of Ickworth, Labourer.

Sept. 13. John son of William & Sophia Cater (late Middleditch) of Horringer, Labourer.

1820. March 1. Elizabeth daughter of John & Mary Hammond (late Stocking) of Ickworth, Labourer.

March 14. Arthur son of James & Mary Cross (late Wallace) of Ickworth, Labourer.

Aug. 27. Elizabeth daughter of John & Mary Winch (late Lanham) of Ickworth, Labourer.

1821. July 15. Elizabeth daughter of John & Mary Finch (late Cobbing) of Ickworth, Groom.

July 22. Henry son of James & Mary Cross (late Wallis) of Ickworth, Labourer.

July 29. Robert son of Robert & Sarah Rolfe (late Farrance) of Ickworth, Gamekeeper.

Sept. 30. Ann daughter of Thomas & Susan Ely (late Manning) of Ickworth, Labourer.

Nov. 10. George Shepherd son of William & Elizabeth Bilson (late Nayler) of Ickworth, Gamekeeper.

1822. June 2. Maria daughter of John & Mary Winch (late Lanham) of Ickworth, Labourer.

1823. June 15. Johnson son of James & Mary Cross (late Wallace) of Ickworth, Labourer.

Oct. 9. Charles Francis son of William & Elizabeth Bilson (late Naylor) of Ickworth, Gamekeeper.

1824. June 27. Sarah Ann daughter of James & Virtue Anderson (late Keeler) of St. Mary's, Bury St. Edmunds, Grocer.

1824. Aug.   8. Harriot Rebecca daughter of Robert & Sarah Rolfe
                  (late Farrance) of Ickworth, Gamekeeper. Born
                  Aug. 31, 1823.

      Dec.   5. Susan daughter of John & Mary Albon (late Clark) of
                  Chevington, Labourer.

1825. April 24. Marianne daughter of Thomas & Ann Avis (late Wright)
                  of Ickworth, Servant.

      Dec.   25. Ann daughter of William & Mary Plum (late Howlett)
                  of Ickworth, Gamekeeper.

1826. July   2. George son of James & Mary Cross (late Wallis) of
                  Ickworth, Labourer. Born July 16, 1825.

      Dec.   3. George son of John & Harriet Short (late Powel) of
                  Horringer, Stonemason. (Entered by mistake.
                  Henry Cherry).

1827. June   24. Phœbe daughter of Robert & Sarah Rolfe (late Far-
                  rance) of Ickworth, Gamekeeper. Born Dec. 8.

      July   5. Ann daughter of William & Mary Plum (late Howlett)
                  of Ickworth, Gamekeeper.

      July   8. Elizabeth Ann daughter of James & Susannah Byford
                  (late Lanham) of Ickworth, Labourer.

      July   8. Thomas son of John & Mary Winch (late Lanham) of
                  Ickworth, Labourer.

      July   15. Harriet daughter of John & Mary Arborn (late Clarke)
                  of Ickworth, Labourer.

      Dec.   18. Elizabeth Maria daughter of James & Maria Howe (late
                  Shore) of Ickworth, Farmer.

1828. Feb.   27. Thomas son of John & Mary Ann Evered (late Arborn)
                  of Martin's Green, Chevington, Labourer.

1829. Feb.   22. William son of Ann Arborn of Ickworth.

      May   17. Maria daughter of William & Mary Plum (late Howlett)
                  of Ickworth, Gamekeeper.

1830. April   6. James Henry son of James & Maria Howe (late Shore)
                  of Ickworth, late Servant.

1830. Oct. 15. Abraham son of James & Sarah Arborn (late Harris) of Ickworth, Labourer.

Oct. 21. Frederick George son of Right Hon. Charles Augustus Ellis, Lord Howard de Walden, Baron, & Lady Lucy (late Bentinck) of Ickworth. Born Aug. 9.

Dec. 25. Elizabeth daughter of Edward & Sarah Crack (late Lanham) of Ickworth, Labourer.

1832. May 22. Sarah daughter of William & Mary Plumb (late Howlet) of Ickworth, Gamekeeper.

Sept. 29. Adelaide, daughter of Right Hon. Frederick William, Earl Jermyn, & the Lady Katharine Isabella Hervey, (late Manners), of Ickworth, Born Feb. 20.

Oct. 18. Sarah daughter of Edward & Sarah Crack (late Langham) of Ickworth, Labourer.

Dec. 30. Anne daughter of James & Maria Howe (late Shore) of Ickworth, late Gamekeeper.

1833. Sept. 8. George Evered son of John & Mary Langham (late Evered) of Ickworth, Labourer.

Dec. 25. Henry son of James & Frances Cross (late Clary) of Ickworth, Labourer.

1834. March 16. Ann daughter of James & Sarah Arborn (late Harris) of Ickworth, Labourer.

May 18. Jeremiah son of James & Sophia Mayhew (late Simkin) of Ickworth Park, Labourer.

Sept. 30. Augusta Georgiana Sophia daughter of Frederick Seymour Esq. & the Lady Augusta Seymour (late Hervey) of Brighton. Born Aug. 19.

1835. April 19. George son of Edward & Sarah Crack (late Langham) of Ickworth, Labourer.

Dec. 25. Jane daughter of James & Frances Cross (late Clary) of Ickworth, Labourer.

1836. May 22. Emma daughter of James & Sarah Arborn, of Ickworth, Labourer.

1836. July   10. William Burton, son of William & Sarah Paine, of Ickworth, Carpenter.

1837. May   14. Edward son of Edward & Sarah Crack, of Ickworth, Labourer.

June   11. Hannah daughter of William & Mary Plumb, of Thetford, Keeper. Privately baptized Aug. 6, 1836.

Sept.   8. Augustus Henry Charles, son of Frederick William, Earl Jermyn, & Katharine Isabella Hervey (late Manners) of Ickworth.

Oct.   20. Emily daughter of James & Sophia Mayhew (late Simkin) of Ickworth Park, Labourer.

Dec.   25. John Thomas son of James & Frances Cross (late Clary) of Ickworth Park, Labourer,

1838. Jan.   28. Arthur John son of William & Sarah Paine (late Anderson) of Ickworth, Carpenter.

March 22. William son of James & Sarah Arborn (late Harris) of Ickworth, Labourer.

May   6. Isaac son of Richard & Mary Anne Harris (late Boreham) of Ickworth, Labourer.

1839. May   10. William James son of James & Frances Cross (late Clarey) of Chevington, Labourer.

Sept.   22. Jane daughter of Edward & Sarah Crack (late Langham) of Ickworth, Labourer.

Nov.   17. William John son of John & Marianne Cross (late Willingham) of Ickworth, Labourer.

1840. June   9. Sarah daughter of Richard & Mary Harris (late Boreham) of Chevington, Labourer.

June   9. Sophia & James twin children of James & Sophia Mayhew (late Simkin) of Chevington, Labourer. Born May 2.

July   19. Rose Ann daughter of John & Elizabeth Smith (late Payne) of Chevington, Gamekeeper.

1840. Aug. 2. Harriet daughter of James & Maria Peachey (late Jennison) of Chevington, Bailiff.

Nov. 29. Jane daughter of Marianne Hunt, of Chevington.

Dec. 6. John Frederick Arthur son of Rev. Lord Arthur Charles and Patience Hervey (late Singleton) of Ickworth. Born Nov. 11.

Dec. 27. James Thomas son of James & Mary Bradford (late Bilson) of Newmarket, Studgroom.

1841 June 20. Charles son of James & Frances Cross (late Clary) of Chevington, Labourer.

1842. Feb. 13. Sarah Elizabeth Harriet daughter of Rev. Lord Arthur Charles & Patience Hervey (late Singleton) of Ickworth. Born Jan 13.

March 13. James son of John & Mary Anne Cross (late Willingham) of Ickworth, Labourer.

June 26. Thomas son of Edward & Sarah Crack (late Lanham) of Ickworth, Labourer.

Sept. 25. William Frederick son of John & Elizabeth Smith (late Payne) of Chevington, Gamekeeper.

1843. May 14. Thomas son of James & Maria Peachey (late Jennison) of Chevington, Land-bailiff. Born Feb. 28, 1842.

May 21. Mary daughter of James & Eliza Finch (late Parratt) of Chevington, Farmer.

July 2. Eliza daughter of Richard & Mary Anne Harris (late Boreham) of Chevington, Labourer.

Aug. 13. Thomas son of James & Frances Cross (late Clary) of Chevington, Labourer.

Oct. 1. Adeliza Georgiana daughter of Frederick William, Earl Jermyn, & Lady Katharine Isabella Hervey (late Manners) of Ickworth. Born Aug. 17.

1844. May 5. Susannah daughter of John & Elizabeth Smith (late Payne) of Chevington, Gamekeeper.

1844. May   19. Alfred son of James & Sophia Mayhew (late Simkin) of Chevington, Labourer.

June   2. Emily daughter of John & Mary Ann Cross (late Willingham) of Chevington, Labourer.

Oct.   6. Henry William son of Robert & Maria Wallace (late Malt) of Chevington, Labourer.

1845. March   2. James son of James & Sarah Arborn (late Harris) of Chevington, Labourer.

June   1. Eliza daughter of James & Eliza Finch (late Parratt) of Chevington, Farmer.

June   1. Henrietta daughter of Joseph & Henrietta Maidment (late Pond) of Chevington, Gamekeeper.

June   15. David son of Edward & Sarah Crack (late Langham) of Ickworth, Labourer.

Sept.   7. Mary Katharine Isabella daughter of Frederick William, Earl Jermyn, & Lady Katharine Hervey (late Manners) of Ickworth.

1846. Jan.   4. John son of John and Elizabeth Smith (late Paine) of Chevington, Gamekeeper.

Jan.   18. Frederick son of James & Maria Peachey (late Jennison) of Chevington, Land Bailiff.

May   31. Susan daughter of Robert & Maria Wallace (late Malt) of Chevington, Labourer.

Nov.   22. Francis son of Frederick William, Earl Jermyn, & Lady Katharine Isabella Hervey (late Manners) of Ickworth.

Dec.   26. Henry son of John & Marianne Cross (late Willingham) of Chevington, Labourer.

1847. Jan.   17. Sydenham Henry Augustus son of Rev. Lord Arthur Charles & Patience Hervey (late Singleton) of Ickworth. Born Dec. 20, 1846.

May   23. Henry son of John & Elizabeth Smith (late Payne) of Chevington, Game keeper.

1847. Aug. 22. Jane Anna daughter of George & Emily Arbon (late Claydon) of Ickworth, Labourer.

Sept. 5. Jane Elizabeth daughter of George & Jane Rolfe (late Hunt) of Ickworth, Coachman.

1848. Sept. 10. George Thomas son of George & Jane Rolfe (late Hunt) of Ickworth, Coachman.

Dec. 3. Alfred Greville Howard son of Lord Alfred & Sophy Hervey (late Chester) of Ickworth. Born Nov. 7.

Dec. 17. James Howe son of John & Elizabeth Smith (late Paine) of Chevington, Gamekeeper.

Dec. 24. Ellen Elizabeth daughter of James & Maria Peachey (late Jennison) of Chevington, Land Bailiff.

Dec. 31. Katharine Patience Georgiana daughter of Rev. Lord Arthur Charles & Patience Hervey (late Singleton) of Ickworth. Born Dec. 2

1849, Sept. 23. Anniss daughter of George & Emily Arbon (late Clayton) of Ickworth, Labourer.

1850. Jan. 6. Johnson son of John & Marianne Cross (late Willingham), of Chevington, Labourer.

Jan. 26. Arthur son of Rev. Lord Arthur Charles & Patience Hervey (late Singleton), of Ickworth. Born the same day.

Aug, 12. Edith Mary daughter of Charles Francis & Edith Bilson (late Roberts), of Ickworth, Gamekeeper.

1851. Oct. 26. Algernon Charles George son of Lord Alfred & Sophy Hervey (late Chester), of Ickworth. Born Sept. 28.

Nov. 30. Arthur Henry Wriothesley, son of Rev. Lord Arthur Charles & Patience Hervey, (late Singleton), of Ickworth. Born Nov. 3.

Dec. 7. Richard Lawrence, son of William & Anna Finch (late Orpen), both deceased, of Southwood Park near Hargrave, Farmer. Born March 27.

D

1852. March 28. Isaac son of Robert & Maria Wallace (late Malt) of Chevington, Iron Gates, Labourer.

June   6. George son of John & Marianne Cross (late Willingham), of Chevington, Labourer.

Aug.   22. William son of John & Emma Eley (late Harris), of Chevington, Labourer.

Oct.   3. Ada Elizabeth daughter of George & Susan Goss (late Poley) of Ickworth, Labourer.

1853. May   15. Patience daughter of Robert & Maria Wallace (late Malt), of Chevington, Labourer.

Sept. 11. Patience Mary daughter of Rev. Lord Arthur Charles & Patience Hervey (late Singleton) of Ickworth. Born July 21.

Oct.   2. Eleanor Marie daughter of Pierre Benjamin & Catherine Desnaux (late Coe) of Ickworth, Valet. Born Dec. 15. 1852.

1854. Jan.   1. Elizabeth daughter of Jonathan & ——— Race (late Richardson) of Ickworth, Labourer.

Nov.   12. James Arthur son of Rev. Lord Arthur Charles & Patience Hervey (late Singleton) of Ickworth.

Dec.   25. Charles son of John & Marianne Cross (late Willingham) of Ickworth, Martin's Green, Labourer.

1855. Aug.   12. Elijah son of Elijah & Amelia Cooke, of Rugby, Engine-driver.

Nov.   18. George son of John & Harriet Cater (late Prince) of Ickworth, Martin's Green, Labourer.

1856. Dec.   14. Maria daughter of Robert & Patience Squibb (late Cooke) of Ickworth, Gardener.

1857. Sept. 13. Caroline Augusta, daughter of Rev. Lord Arthur Charles & Patience Hervey (late Singleton) of Ickworth. Born July 7.

1857. Sept. 20. Thomas Prince son of John & Harriett Cator (late Prince) of Ickworth, Gardener's man.

Dec. 13. Emily daughter of Robert & Patience Squibbs (late Cook of Ickworth, Gardener.

Dec. 25. John son of John & Marianne Cross (late Willingham) of Ickworth, Martin's Green, Labourer.

1858. Aug. 1. Mary Ann daughter of Charles Francis & Edith Bilson (late Roberts) of Horringer, Park-keeper.

Sept. 19. Francis Benjamin son of Pierre Benjamin & Catherine Desnaux (late Coe) of Ickworth, Servant.

Nov. 14. Alfred son of Robert & Maria Wallis (late Malt) of Chevington, Labourer.

Nov. 28. Felicité daughter of Robert & Patience Squibbs (late Cook) of Ickworth, Gardener.

1859. March 6. Arthur Benjamin son of Benjamin & Sarah Last (late Frost) of Ickworth, Gamekeeper.

May 22. Thomas son of Thomas & Elizabeth Mitchell (late Plum) of Ickworth, Servant.

June 9. George son of William & Mary Ann Evered (late Betts) of Horsepool, Chevington, Garden man.

Aug. 7. Frederica Mary Lucy, daughter of Rev. Lord Arthur Charles & Patience Hervey (late Singleton) of Ickworth. Born July 10.

1860. Jan. 29. Elizabeth Mary daughter of John & Harriett Cater (late Prince) of Ickworth, Gardener's man.

April 15. Patience Mary daughter of Robert & Patience Squibbs (late Cook) of Ickworth, Gardener.

April 29. Mary Ann daughter of Julian & Ellen Sharp (late Brown) of Ickworth, Labourer.

May 27. Ellen daughter of John & Mary Ann Cross (late Willingham) of Chevington, Labourer.

1860   Aug.   5. Jessie daughter of Jonathan & Emma Race (late
              Richardson) of Ickworth, Labourer.

1861. July   12. Emma daughter of George & Susan Goss (late Pooly) of
              Ickworth, Labourer.

       Sept. 15. Eliza daughter of Robert & Patience Squibbs (late Cook)
              of Ickworth, Gardener.

1862. July   6. Thomas John son of Charles Francis & Edith Bilson
              (late Roberts) of Horringer, Park-keeper.

       Aug.   10. Jonathan son of Jonathan & Emma Race (late Richardson)
              of Ickworth, Labourer.

       Aug.   24. Charlotte daughter of Robert & Patience Squibbs (late
              Cook) of Ickworth, Gardener.

1863. Aug.   16. Sarah daughter of John & Harriett Cater (late Prince)
              of Chevington, Labourer.

       Oct.   25. Robert Humphrey son of Robert & Patience Squibbs
              (late Cook) of Ickworth, Gardener.

1864. Feb.   21. Katherine Adine Geraldine, daughter of Frederick
              William John & Geraldine Mary Georgiana Hervey
              (late Anson), Earl & Countess Jermyn, of Ickworth.
              Born Jan. 15.

       March 20. Frederick son of Jonathan & Emma Race (late
              Richardson) of Ickworth, Labourer.

       June   12. Elizabeth Agnes daughter of Charles Francis & Edith
              Bilson (late Roberts) of Horringer, Park keeper.

       Aug.   21. Lionel Maling son of William Maling & Lilly Wynch
              (late Wilde) of Horringer, Esquire.

1865. Sept. 24. Rosetta daughter of Robert & Patience Squibbs (late
              Cook) of Ickworth, Gardener.

1866. Feb.   11. Edward Robinson son of James & Elizabeth Dadley (late
              Robinson) of Ickworth, Gamekeeper.

       May   6. Adelaide daughter of William & Rebecca Bailey (late
              Evered) of Ickworth, Labourer.

1866. June 3. George Wynyard Colvile and Alexandra Gruinard, children of Wynard & Margaret Ellen Battye, (late Colvile) of Horringer, Captain in Bengal Army, were received into the Church. Born & Baptized in India, the one on Sept. 3, 1862, May 3, 1863, the other on April, 29, 1865, May 28, 1865.

July 29. Rebecca Kate daughter of Frederic & Catherine Last (late Wallis) of Ickworth, Coachman.

Oct. 28. Rosa Maria daughter of Thomas & Frances Edwards (late Deacon) of Ickworth, Carpenter.

1867. March 5. Frederick George Robinson, son of James & Elizabeth Dadley (late Robinson) of Ickworth, Gamekeeper.

March 10. John Edward son of John & Harriet Cater, (late Prince) of Chevington, Garden labourer.

April 7. John son of Jonathan & Emma Race (late Richardson) of Ickworth, Labourer.

Dec. 8. Charlotte Elizabeth daughter of Richard & Louisa Howlett (late Sore) of Ickworth, Gamekeeper.

1868. May 3. Walter Frederick son of Frederick & Catherine Last (late Wallace) of Ickworth, Coachman.

June 7. Frederick Robinson, son of James & Elizabeth Dadley (late Robinson) of Ickworth, Gamekeeper.

1869. April 11. Melinda daughter of Richard & Louisa Howlett (late Sore) of Ickworth, Gamekeeper.

Oct. 17. Edward Herbert son of Frederick & Catherine Last (late Wallis) of Ickworth, Coachman.

Oct. 24. Fanny daughter of James & Elizabeth Dadley (late Robinson) of Ickworth, Game-keeper.

1870. March 13. William John, son of Charles Martin & Emily Cockbill (late Cross) of City Road, London, Sergeant.

April 24. Florence Ellen daughter of Robert & Patience Squibbs (late Cook) of Ickworth, Gardener.

1870. July   24. William Blythe son of William Hide & Mary Ann
                    Dadley (late Blythe) of Ickworth, Gamekeeper.

1871. July   9. Herbert, son of James & Elizabeth Dadley, of Ickworth,
                    Game-keeper.

       Sept.   3. Adela Constance, daughter of Charles & Emily Martin,
                    of Ickworth, Soldier.

       Nov.   24. Sarah Elizabeth, daughter of William Hide & Mary Ann
                    Dadley, of Ickworth, Gamekeeper.

       Nov.   24. Thomas Henry, son of William Hide & Mary Ann
                    Dadley, of Ickworth, Gamekeeper.

1872. (no date.) John Cracknell, son of Samuel & Emma Clowe, of
                    Ickworth, Coachman.

       Nov.   3. Dick Fred, son of Richard & Louise Howlett, of Ickworth,
                    Gamekeeper.

1873. Feb.   8. Ellen, daughter of James & Elizabeth Dadley, of
                    Ickworth, Gamekeeper.

       March   9. James, son of William Hide & Mary Ann Dadley, of
                    Ickworth, Gamekeeper.

       March 31. Herbert William, son of Herbert & Caroline Mary
                    Pepper, of Little Saxham, (Ickworth Park) Game-
                    keeper.

       Aug.   31. William Edward, son of Richard & Louisa Howlett, of
                    Ickworth, Gamekeeper.

1874. April   27. Alice Adeliza, daughter of Frederick William John
                    Marquis of Bristol & Geraldine Mary Georgiana
                    Hervey (late Anson) of Ickworth.

       May   24. Herbert, son of Frederick & Susan Vincent, of Ickworth
                    Park, Chevington, Labourer.

       May   24. Ann Haddon, daughter of Josiah & Ann Warren, of
                    Long Buckley, Northampton, Railway Pointsman.

       May   24. William Walter, son of Josiah & Ann Warren.

1874. May   24. Gertrude Amelia, daughter of Josiah & Ann Warren.

      May   24. Sarah Elizabeth, daughter of Josiah & Ann Warren.

      June 14. Frederick Walter, son of Charles Martin & Emily Cockbill, of Finsbury, Middlesex, Militia Sergeant.

      July 19. Charles, son of William Hide & Mary Ann Dadley, of Ickworth, Gamekeeper.

      Aug. 30. Emma, daughter of James & Elizabeth Dadley, of Ickworth, Gamekeeper.

1875. Aug.   1. Carry, daughter of Herbert & Caroline Mary Pepper, of Little Saxham, Ickworth Park, Gamekeeper.

      Dec. 26. Helen Edith, daughter of Charles Martin & Emily Cockbill, Militia Barracks, City Road, London, Staff Sergeant.

1876. Feb. 13. Maude Mary, daughter of James & Elizabeth Dadley, of Ickworth, Gamekeeper.

1877. April 8. Sarah Jane, daughter of Frederick & Susan Vincent, of Ickworth Park, Under Gardener.

      June 24. Minnie Jemima, daughter of James & Elizabeth Dadley of Ickworth Park, Head Gamekeeper.

      Sept. 16. Annie Louisa, daughter of George & Louisa Cross of Ickworth Park, Pensioner.

      Sept. 16 Edgar, son of Alice Race, of Ickworth Park, Servant.

1878. Feb. 24. Susanah, daughter of William Hide & Mary Ann Dadley, of Ickworth Park, Gamekeeper.

1879. July 13. Minnie Rose, daughter of George & Louisa Cross, of Dalham, Suffolk, Pensioner.

1881. July 24. Harry, son of Charles & Emily Cockbill, of Poplar, London, Timekeeper.

      Dec.   4. Arthur Harry, son of Frederick & Susan Vincent, of Ickworth Park, Chevington, Gardener.

1883. April 22. Louisa, daughter of Herbert & Caroline Mary Pepper, of Ickworth, Gamekeeper.

1883. May   6. Ada, daughter of Isaac & Anne Wallace, of Chevington,
                   Gamekeeper.

       June   3. William Richard, son of George & Louisa Cross, of
                   Hargrave, Suffolk, Pensioner.

1884. March 30. Flora Adelaide, daughter of George & Jessie Bailey, of
                   Ickworth Park, Chevington, Groom.

1886. May   2. Hilda Jessie, daughter of George & Jessie Bailey, of
                   Ickworth Park, Chevington, Groom.

1887. July   3. Sydney William, son of George & Jessie Bailey, of
                   Ickworth Park, Chevington, Groom.

1890. April 20. Vivian Mary, daughter of Henry & Emma Flack, of
                   Ickworth Park, Chevington, Gardener.

MARRIAGES.

1566.	July	9.	John Sterne	&	Mary Barret.
1567.	June	3.	Edward Barret	&	Mary Sterne.
1569.	April	25.	William Lynge	&	Mary Spalding.
	May	8.	William Langly	&	Agnes ———— .
1570.	Jan.	2.	William Alington Esq.	&	Mary Worlich.
1572.	July	6.	William Bronne	&	Rose Frost.
	Nov.	16.	John Langly	&	Tabitha Spalding.
1575.	July	24.	William Pettitt	&	Elizabeth Paman.
	Nov.	3.	James Crekk	&	Bridget Meyhew.
1576.	Nov.	4.	Thomas Galt	&	Barbara Spalding.
1578.	Feb.	6.	Philip Pole	&	Barbara Fyne.
1579.	June	28.	John Costard	&	Ame West.
1582.	Jan.	12.	Edward Silverson	&	Bridget ———— .
	May	24.	John Linge	&	Isabel Hurst.
	Sept.	16.	John Hervey	&	Frances Bokkyng.
1583.	May	20.	John Mud	&	Mary Barnes.
	Oct.	21.	Peter Dege	&	Melysent Paman.
	Nov.	3.	John Dowsing	&	Rachel Sage.
1584.	Aug.	30.	Robert Bullok	&	Fortune Woodly.
	Nov.	10.	Henry Colleng	&	Bridget Harvey.
1585.	Aug.	8.	Robert————	&	Jane Gellot.
1588.	July	9.	John Buckenham	&	Jone Eldred.
	July	22.	Richard Evered	&	Margaret Wilson.
	Aug.	6.	Edward Chansfeild	&	Elizabeth Rene.
1590.	Oct.	4.	Francis Spalding	&	Mary Weeb.
	Oct.	26.	William Olleett	&	Agnes Lylly.
1593.	Oct.	17.	Edward Sponely	&	Agnes Wasp.

E

1595.	Oct.	16.	Robert Brant	&	Elizabeth Wadelo.
1596.	June	24.	Thomas Troutten	&	Joane Simsen.
1597.	Sept.	21.	Ollifer Steele	&	Elizabeth Linge.
	Oct.	24.	William Gallant	&	Anne Standly.
1598.	April	25.	Mathew Tomson	&	Dorothe Paske.
	Nov.	1.	Gregorie Carter	&	Alice Withers.
1601.	June	1.	Thomas Payton	&	Isbell Linge.
1604.	Oct.	7.	John Parker	&	Elizabeth Linge.
1606.	Nov.	17.	John Gaskinne	&	Bridget Spincke.
1607.			William Hilles	&	Mary Withers.
1609.	Oct.	18.	John Waterhouse	&	Lucresse Wadelow.
	Nov.	20.	Andrew Thredder	&	Margarett Risbie.
1610	May	24.	John Firminne	&	Audry Linge.
	June	10.	John Harison	&	Anne Diggle.
1613.	Oct.	18.	Edward Linge	&	Anne Norman.
1615.	Feb.	12.	Josias Sillett	&	Margarett Bontene.
1619.	Jan.	31.	Robert Manning	&	Ellen Godfry.
1620.	Oct.	4.	Robert Verbye	&	Anne ffilbridge.
1621.	Dec.	9.	James Baylie	&	Dine Talbot.
1623.	Oct.	6.	Robert Hamond	&	Mary Hempson.
1624.	June	28.	Henery Pammant	&	Anne Payton.
1626.	June	22.	Reynold Whayman	&	Martha Bowtell
1627.	Nov.	30.	George Hibble	&	Winifred Reeve.
	Feb.	7.	John Warner	&	Rebecca Grange.
1628.	Feb.	3.	Richard Bayley	&	Alice Simson.
1632.	June	6.	Richard Spenser.	&	Susan Hibble.
	Sept.	21.	Hugh Spenser	&	Mary Rogers.
	Sept.	27.	Robert Jobson	&	Elizabeth Edwards.
1633.	April	14.	Arthur Cutterice	&	Elizabeth Goose.
1634.	June	10.	John Waterhouse	&	Amie Jakes.
1636.	May	11.	John Blounder	&	Margaret Boyden.
	Feb.	21.	Edward Stone	&	Rose Milby.

1637.	Oct.	25.	William Syer	&	Elizabeth Godfrey.
1638.	Nov.	27.	John Vales	&	Judeth Merrylls.
	Jan.	18.	Thomas Avis	&	Thomazin Dowe.
1639.	June	3.	George Shippe	&	Judeth Brooke.
1640.	Nov.	2.	Robert Day	&	Audrey Ellit.
	Feb.	2.	Thomas Bird	&	Sarah Redging.
1642.	July	21.	John Stannard	&	Margery Miles.
1647.	Oct.	9.	Arthur Goodchild	&	Susan Goldsmith
1651.	July	24.	Robert Crosse	&	Mary Eliot.
	July	26.	John Barter	&	Mary Dale.
	Jan.	6.	John Huggons	&	Elizabeth Risbie.
1652.	March	3.	William Handler	&	Jone Sillet.
1653.	May	30.	John Craske	&	Alice Wragge.
1655.	July	30.	Mr. James Reynolds	&	Mrs. Judeth Hervey.
1657.	Jan.	31.	John Simons	&	Elizabeth Casen.
1658.	July	21.	Mr. Thomas Hervey	&	Mis. Isabella May.
	Sept.	23.	John Parman	&	Sarah Brook.
	Dec.	17.	William Adams	&	Alice Cooke.
	March	3.	Jasper Blemmell	&	Anne Goodrick.
1659.	May	12.	Thomas Johnson	&	Grace Whiting.
	Jan.	4.	Edward ffincham	&	Alice Border.
	Feb.	9.	Richard Umbletam	&	Anne Turner.
1660.	Oct.	4.	Nicholas Sargeant	&	Mary Pammant.
1661.	July	25.	William Smith	&	Elizabeth Turner.
1662.	July	3.	John Crysall	&	Anne Gardner.
	Nov.	3.	Thomas Smith	&	Mary Palke.
1663.	Nov.	12.	Abraham Bennall	&	Martha Sherman.
1665.	April	3.	John Cricke	&	Mary ffrank.
	Aug.	2.	John ffarrar	&	Alice Wiseman.
	Aug.	17.	John Parker	&	Grace Nelson.
	Sept.	25.	ffrancis ffrost	&	ffrances Reeve.
1666.	Aug.	30.	Randolfe Locke	&	Bridget ffrost.

1667.	April	17.	Robert Nun	&	ffrances Wiffin.
	July	30.	William Fflatt	&	Barbara Emins.
1668.	Aug.	16.	Thomas Cooke	&	Anne Baythorn.
	Oct.	29.	John Turner	&	Mary Smith.
	Feb.	14.	Thomas Kinge	&	Elizabeth Warde.
1669.	Dec.	16.	Mr. Thomas Johnson Cler	&	Mrs. Anne Leming.
1672.	Sept.	19.	Samuell Reeve	&	Mary Goodchild.
	Nov.	19.	Edward Cooke	&	Alice Livermore.
	Jan.	13.	Thomas Chaplin	&	Mary Goodine.
1674.	Oct.	17.	Christopher Prick	&	Susan Last.
	Oct.	20.	John Rolph	&	Mary Potter.
1675.	Oct.	14.	Robert ffrost	&	Mary Collins.
1676.	Nov.	7.	Edward Chevely	&	Susan Thorne.
	Nov.	30.	Joshua Horax	&	Alice Dickson.
	Jan.	30.	Arthur Goodchild	&	Sarah Paman.
1677.	Sept.	25.	James Weyard	&	Elizabeth Stratton.
1679.	May	7.	John Bullbrook	&	Anne Spencer.
	May	15.	William Martin	&	Dorothy Cabeck.
	Jan.	11.	William Warren	&	Christian Billum.
	Feb.	18.	John Brook	&	Joanna Prat.
1681.	Aug.	18.	Henery Abbot	&	Elizabeth Turner.
	Sept.	14.	Mr. Robert Underwood	&	Mis : Margaret Chaplin.
	March	16.	John Nun	&	Anne Glanvel.
1682.	Oct.	1.	Abraham Underwood,	Clericus, & Mis : Elizabeth Underwood.	
	Oct.	2.	Thomas Murton	&	Abigal Dogget.
	Oct.	31.	Alexander Oswal	&	Mary Reinolds.
1684.	Sept.	4.	John Brewster	&	Elizabeth Guy.
	Nov.	13.	John Godfrey	&	Lidea Goar.
	Nov.	24.	Mr. Thomas Chaplin	&	Margaret Wright.
1685.	Nov.	1.	Robert Loker	&	Susan Segrave.
	Feb.	11.	Thomas Rose	&	Margaret Chapline.

1686.	April	13.	John Smith	& Mary Robinson.
1689.	May	21.	Thomas Stade	& Ann Bullbrook.
1690.			(Blank)	
1692.	Sept.	28.	Hugh Spencer	& Alice Adams.
	Oct.	2.	Edmund Hollax	& ffebe Bradbruck.

1693. Aug. 13. Thomas Bulbrook of Whepstead & Martha Garwood of Hawstead.

Sept. 28. Henry Hollod & Marget Sparrow, both of Ickworth.

Nov. 21. James Silvester of St. Maries Parish in St. Edmunds Bury & Elizabeth Holden of Hasted.

1695. Aug. 8. John Potter & Sarah Ballard, both of Great Saxham.

Aug. 29. Joseph Alexander & Frances Martin, both of St. Edmunds Bury.

Jan. 13. Thomas Ling & Christian Ames, both of this Parish.

1696. March 29. John Vale of Nayland in Suffolk & Ann Alexander of Horsely in Essex.

April 20. Isaac Allwinkle of Lavenham in Suffolk & Elizabeth Bridgeman of Ickworth.

Sept. 29. James Frost of Horninsheth & Elizabeth Hood of Ickworth.

1697. July 27. George Rattly of Hawsted & Mary Redgen of Chevington.

1698. Oct. 27. Thomas Manning of Sinkles Bradfield & Mary Hood of Ickworth.

1699. Sept. 26. John Novel, Clerk, & Mrs. Mary Short, both of St. Edmunds Bury.

1700. Aug. 23. Mr. Benjamin Malfalgueyrat, Chirurgion, & Mrs. Mary Harris, both of St. Edmunds Bury.

Sept. 13. Nathan Booty of Lackford & Margaret Cooke of Whepsted.

1701. May   15.   Mr. Richard Benskin, Rector of Little Saxham, & Mrs. Hannah Rich of Bardwell.

Nov.   2.   John Houlden   & Abigail Spark, both of Hasted.

Dec.   25.   Christopher Spight of Great Whelnetham & Ann Harrold of St. Edmonds Bury.

1702. Oct.   6.   Francis Shaw of Horninsheth & Alice Ewin.

Oct.   14.   Robert Sandcroft of Ickworth & Mary Mason of Freckenham.

Nov.   12.   Richard Everard   & Elizabeth Skinner, both of Ickworth.

1703. Oct.   21.   John Ery of Stansfield & Ann Kemp of Chevington.

1704. June   23.   Thomas Spencely, Gentleman, & Mrs. Sarah Lancaster, both of Bury St. Edmunds.

1705. May   28.   John Abbot, of Mildenhall, Gentleman, & Mrs. Frances Cook of Whepsted.

1707. June   9.   John Howlet of Exning & Mary Hewes of this town

1709. June   16.   Mr. Robert Sturgeon, of Bury St. Edmunds, single man, & Mrs. Betty Steward, of Whepsted, single woman.

July   12.   Mr. John Blomfield & Mrs. Ann Ling, both of St. Edmunds Bury, both Single.

Sept.   18.   John Steward & Ann Pain, both of Chevington, both Single.

Jan.   22.   Robert Ling & Elizabeth Gootch, both of Horninsheth both Single.

1712. Sept.   4.   Thomas Elms of Ickworth & Sarah Norman of Brockly.

1713. Oct.   6.   Tuesday, Robert Fisk, Gentleman, & Margaret Steward, Gentlewoman, both Single persons of ye Town of Whepsted.

1716. Sept. 27.   Mr. Robert Wolf of Hasted & Mrs. Ann Eldred of Denson, both Single.

1718. April 25.   Arthur Goodchild of this town, Widower, & Frances Curchin, Widow.

1718. May 25. George Helder, of Ampton, & Elizabeth Summer of this Town, both Single.

Oct. 12. John Living & Ann Manning, both of Rougham and Single.

1719. Sept. 22. Thomas Nunn, Widower, & Elizabeth Clews, Single, both of this Town.

1720. Feb. 2. Mr. William Oliver, of Ickworth, & Mrs. Ann Webster, of Newmarket, both Single.

1722. Oct. 21. John Harrold & Ann Everard, both of Bury and Single.

Nov. 6. William Brian of Hawsted & Sarah Pettit of Ickworth, both Single.

1723. Dec. 26. Walter Pain & Christiana Tuor.

Feb. 17. Mr. John Young & Susan Leaver, both of Bury St. Edmunds.

1724. May 7. William Brinkley & Mary Couzens, both of Bury St. Edmunds.

Sept. 6. Roger Cuzens & Dabene (?) Cornwill.

1728. May 31. Mr. William Simkins & Mrs. Ann Nelson of Newmarkett.

Nov. 20. William Hedle & Ann Cragman.

1729. May 11. John Griblen & Cathren Sparck, both of Wapsted.

1730. Sept. 10. Thomas Robinson, of Sudbury, & Mary Raven of Bury St. Edmonds.

1731. Sept. 23. Sir Robart Smith & the Lady Luazer Harvey.

1733. Aug. 22. John Wanner & Elizabeth Hedle.

1738. March 6. James Morley of Barham, Singleman, & Marian Gentleman, widow, of this Parish, by License.

1739. Oct. 5. Robert Latham & Elizabeth Priest, both of Eye and Single, by License.

1740. Dec. 31. The Hon. & Rev. Mr. Charles Hervey, Rector of this Parish, & Miss Martha Maria Howard of Bury, both Single, by License.

1742. Dec.   16. Mr Edward Drew, of Chedburgh, & Mrs Susan Deecks, of Brockley, both single, by License.

1743. Sept.   29, Thomas Maxham, of Great Saxham, widower, & Ann Mayes, of this Parish, Single woman, by banns.

1744. Jan.   16. Stephen How, widower, of Norton, & Elizabeth Nun, widow, of St Mary's in Bury St Edmunds, by License.

1746/7 Jan.   7. Edward Otley, of Great Saxham, & Elizabeth Baker, of Ickworth, both Single, by License.

1749/50. Feb. 27. Houghton Bailey, of Chevington, & Dinah Emmett, of Ickworth, both Single, by License.

1750. July   8. Samuel Fenton, of Risby, & Elizabeth Sharp, of Chedburgh, by banns.

      Aug.   30. Thomas Scotman, of Newmarket, widower & Mary Mills, of Bury St. Edmunds, Spinster, by License.

1753. Oct.   9. William Simpson, of Reed, & Mercy Blye, of Nolton, both Single, by License.

1758. July   4. Robert Bridges, widower, & Elizabeth Wixon, Single woman, both of this Parish, by License.

1759. Nov.   20. John Everred & Rose Crick, both Single and of this Parish, by Banns.

1760. Sept.   5. Robert Frost of Horningsheath & Sarah Everet, of Ickworth, both Single, by License.

1763. Jan.   16. Robert Stocking of Ickworth & Martha Thorogood, of Ousden, both Single, by License.

1772. Aug.   16. John Winch, widower, & Mary Tillson, single woman, both of Ickworth, by License.

1788. Jan.   8. John Crick, of Chedburgh, & Mary Ward, of Ickworth, both Single, by banns.

1790. July   30. Thomas Evered & Mabel Steed, both of Ickworth & Single, by banns.

1793. Jan.   10. John Double jun., of Horningsheath, & Elizabeth Steed, of Ickworth, both Single, by License.

1795. Oct. 26. Robert Frost, Widower, & Ann Crick, Single, both of Whepsted.

1797. Aug. 21. John Bullet, of Horringer, & Ann Ward, of Ickworth, both Single, by banns.

Sept. 2. Robert Burroughs, of Horningsheath, & Isabella Manning, of Ickworth, both Single, by banns.

1800. Dec. 31. William Bunn, of St Mary's, Bury St. Edmunds, widower, & Susan Hart, of Ickworth, Spinster, by License.

1801. Nov. 24. William Haslewood, of Horringer, & Diana Cocksill, of Ickworth, both Single, by banns.

Dec. 31. William Sier & Susanna Prick, both of Ickworth and Single, by banns.

1802. Feb. 11. Roger Adams, of Horningsheath, & Sophia Aves, of Ickworth, both Single, by License.

Feb. 22. Alexander Riach, of Hardwick, & Ann Wells, of Ickworth, both Single, by License.

1804. Jan. 19. John Hammond, of Whepstead, & Mary Stocking, of Ickworth, both Single, by License.

Nov. 1. John Wade, of Mansel St, London, & Frances Turner, of Ickworth, both Single, by License.

Dec. 6. Thomas Lynnards & Ann Green, both of Ickworth and Single, by banns.

1807. Nov. 25. Benjamin Mason & Mary Johnson, both of Ickworth and Single, by banns.

1808. June 13. John Worlledge, of Ingham, & Mary Ann Shillito, of Ickworth, Spinster, by License.

1814. Oct. 17. Samuel Bentick, of Ixworth, & Rebecca Hour, of Ickworth, by banns.

1816. Dec. 3. John Wallace & Susanna Sale, both of Ickworth and Single, by banns.

1819. Aug. 23. John Winch & Mary Langham, both of Ickworth and Single, by banns.

F

1821. July   23. Thomas Avis, widower, & Ann Wright, spinster, both of Ickworth, by License.

1822. Dec.   24. John Albon & Mary Clark, both of Ickworth and Single, by banns.

1823. May   20. Robert Winch & Elizabeth Crow, both of Ickworth and Single, by banns.

1826. Dec.   25. James Byford & Susannah Langham, both of Ickworth and Single, by banns.

1827. Feb.   22. George Lewis West of Chevington & Sally Howe, of Ickworth, both Single, by banns.

1833. July   29. John Langham & Mary Evered, both of Ickworth and Single, by banns.

1835. April 30. James Pope, of St. Mary's, Bury St. Edmunds, & Elizabeth Mary Bilson, of Ickworth, by License.

      May   6. William Paine, of St Mary's, Bury St. Edmunds, & Sarah Anderson, of Ickworth, by License.

1836. May   26. Richard Harris of Ickworth, & Mary Ann Boreham, of Horningsheath, by banns.

1838. Feb.   3. John Clary, of Little Saxham, & Sophia Fakes, both residing at the boundaries of Ickworth & Little Saxham, by banns.

      March 1. James Bradford, of Horseheath, Co. Cambridge, & Mary Susannah Bilson, of Ickworth, both Single, by License.

1846. Feb.   5. James Bartholomew, of Newmarket, jockey, & Matilda Bilson, of Ickworth, both Single.

      Sept. 9. George Rolfe, Coachman, & Jane Hunt, both Single and of Ickworth.

1848. June 23. James Crack, of Ickworth, & Ann Cuthbert, of Elmswell, both Single.

1852. Dec. 27. William Berry, of Bruton St, London, bookbinder, & Maria Plum, of Ickworth, both Single.

1854. Dec. 21. John Cater & Harriet Prince, both Single and of Ickworth.

1857. May   11. Robert Cobbin, widower, of Chevington, gamekeeper,
             & Mary Ann Ford, widow, of Ickworth, daughter of
             William Talbot.

1866. July   26. Frederick James Nathaniel Best, of London, Ware-
             houseman, & Jane Hunt, of Ickworth, both Single.

      Nov.   29. Richard Somerset le Poer Trench, Viscount Dunlo, &
             Adeliza Georgiana Hervey, of Ickworth, both Single.

1867. April 9. James Cranford Dadley, Gamekeeper, & Rachel
             Selwood, both Single and of Ickworth.

      Oct. *12. George Duley of Ickworth & Esther Cook, of Horringer,
             both Single.

      Dec.   24. James Eley, bachelor, of Chevington, & Susan Goss,
             widow, of Ickworth, daughter of Isaac Poley.

1872. April 30. Frederick Lawrence, bachelor, & Elizabeth Bilson,
             spinster, both of Ickworth, Servants.

1875. Oct.   2. Charles Garwood, bachelor, of Horringer, & Alice Guy,
             Spinster, of Ickworth.

1876. Nov.   16. George Cross, bachelor, Pensioner from the Police force,
             & Louisa Mary Ann Howlett, spinster, both of
             Ickworth.

1877. March 29. George Instance, bachelor, of Brundon, Essex, & Laura
             Elizabeth Farrants, Spinster, of Ickworth.

1878. July   6. George Gosling Barton, bachelor, of Bury St. Edmunds,
             & Mary Ann Woodford, spinster, of Ickworth.

1879. May   20. Isaac Wallace, widower, of Chevington, & Ann Pike,
             spinster, of Ickworth.

1880. Aug.   26. Charles Neagus, bachelor, of Bury St. Edmunds, &
             Sarah Dadley, spinster, of Ickworth.

1882. April 10. Charles Jolly, bachelor, of Enfield, Co. Middlesex, Game-
             keeper, & Sarah Elizabeth Woodford, spinster, of
             Ickworth.

1883. Oct.   18. Elijah Cook, bachelor, Engineer R.N., & Maria Squibbs,
             spinster, both of Ickworth.

1885. Sept. 17. Frederick John Sharpe, bachelor, of Nowton, & Emma Goss, spinster, of Ickworth.

1886. March 4. Allan Harvey Drummond, bachelor, & Katherine Adine Geraldine Hervey, spinster, of Ickworth.

Nov. 13. Thomas Morley, bachelor, & Jessie. Race, spinster, both of Ickworth.

1887. May 21. John Race, bachelor, of Ickworth, & Emma Nunn, spinster, of Chevington.

Nov. 24. Charles Glynne Earle Welby, bachelor, of Denton, Co. Lincoln, & Maria Louisa Helen Hervey, spinster, of Ickworth.

BURIALS.

1566.	April	3.	John Barret.
1567.	Aug.	24.	Thomas Shepard.
	March	14.	John Oylet.
1568.	Sept.	16.	Anne Ditton.
	Nov.	18.	Nicolas Spalding.
	Dec.	3.	Thomas Camps.
	Dec.	8.	Thomas Shepard.
1570.	May	22.	Thomas Roger.
	Aug.	17.	Edward Paman.
	Sept.	21.	John Paman.
	March	3.	Susan Langlye.
1572.	Jan.	7.	Henery Spalding.
1573.	Sept.	10.	Henery Mayhew.
1574.	July	15.	Thomas Shepard.
1576.	March	19.	Margaret Shepard.
	July	21.	Cutbarte Palye.
1577.	Aug.	26.	John Barrett.
1579.	April	17.	Anne Johnsone.
	Jan.	25.	William Ling.
1581.	Jan.	11.	James Lardgine.
1582.	April	15.	William Hurst.
	Nov.	28.	John Burnese.
1583.	May	3.	Cook's Child.
	June	1.	Thomas King.
	Nov.	18.	Robert Johnson.
	March	19.	Alice Johnson.
1584.	March	18.	ffrancès Barnes.
1586.	Oct.	17.	Thomas Wadelowe.

1587.	July	21.	William Gillot.
	Sept.	25.	ffrances Hervey.
1588.	Aug.	25.	Agnes Mayhew.
1590.	Feb.	4.	Mary Abell.
1592.	Sept.	19.	John Oylet's wife,
	Nov,	2.	William Harvey.
1593.	May	12.	Margaret Mud.
	July	7.	Alice Langly.
	Jan,	10.	Ede Abbot.
1595.	Feb.	13.	Mary Briant.
1596.	Aug.	19.	Thomas Simonds,
1597.	Sept.	22.	William Woodes,
			Mr. Robert Castle.
1598.	Dec.	1.	Elizabeth Barret.
1599.	July	8.	Dorothe Pooley.
1600.	March	20.	Margery Balles,
1601.	May	25.	Robert Briant.
	Aug.	27.	Erasmus Diggle.
	March	21.	Elizabeth Payten.
1603.	Feb.	6.	Thomas Harper.
1604.	Sept.	28.	Elizabeth Gipps.
1606.	April	28.	Henrie Buckenham,
	July	20.	John Buckenham.
1609.	Oct.	17.	William ffrogge.
1612.	June	12.	Elizabeth Cutterice.
1613.	Aug.	6.	Thomas Withers.
	Sept.	6.	Edmund Withers,
	Nov.	6,	Alice Withers.
1615.	May	5.	John Barret.
1616,	March	25.	Mis : Elizabeth Harvie.
	June	7.	Anne Wadelowe.
	Aug.	8.	Martha Boydon,

1618. March 25. Robert Bryant.

Nov. 30. Anne Hervey daughter of Sir William Hervey.

1619. March 29. ffrances daughter of John Hervey Esq.

1620. Nov. 19. Elizabeth Briant.

Feb. 22. ffrances Hervey, wife of John Hervey Esq.

1621. Sept. 11. Anne Baily.

Jan. 20. Mary Mud.

1623. April 22. Elizabeth Harvey.

Dec. 2. Jane Barret.

1624. Dec. 9. Margaret Stearne.

Jan. 7. Henry Ware.

1625. Oct. 14. Robert Waterhouse.

Jan. 10. Katharine Harvey.

1626. June 11. Robert Hammant.

Sept. 4. Mary Allington.

Nov. 8. Richard Ware,

1627. Nov. 29. Margaret Bayly.

1628. Sept. 19. Luke Waterhouse.

March 21. Necolas Harvey.

1629. May 8. William Prick.

1630. July 2. Mr. John Harvey Esq.

Aug. 7. John Steed.

Feb. 4. Sicily the wife of Henry Spenser.

1631. April 16. Anne the wife of William Ellit.

Dec. 30. Henry Spenser.

Jan. 26. Thomas Spenser.

1632. Sept. 16. Henry Hervye sonne of Sir William Hervye.

1634. June 21. Anne Waterhouse.

Dec. 17. William Ellit.

1637. April 28. Robert Hammond.

May 9. Susan Cropley.

Feb. 9. Dame Susan Hervey.

1638.	April	9.	Mary Haylocke.
	Jan.	28.	John Croply.
1639.	Aug.	1.	Susan Sudbury.
1640.	June	8.	Anne Cropley.
	March	4.	Samuell Sudbury.
1641.	May	28.	Mary the wife of Thomas Cater.
	Nov.	26.	Elizabeth fford.
	Dec.	12.	Henry Miles.
	Dec.	20.	Amie Waterhouse and Richard Waterhouse.
1642.	April	23.	Margaret Cropley.
	Sept.	24.	Mr. William Hervey.
			John Wright.
1644.	March	27.	William Sudbury.
	May	5.	Elizabeth Carter.
	June	5.	Sarah Summers.
1645.	Sept.	13.	Thomas Carter.
	Dec.	1.	Mary Billum.
1646.	June	14.	Antony Evatte.
1647.	Aug.	10.	Christian Sparke.
			Eliot.
			Goodwife Spark.
1648.	July	13.	William Ellis, son of John Ellis.
1649.	April	11.	Walter Derisly.
	April	17.	ffrancis Derisly.
	June	2.	Edward Paine.
1650.	March	6.	Edward Goldsmith.
	March	13.	Susan Barret.
1651.	April	6.	Thomas Mayhew.
	May	9.	Thomas Mayhew sonne of John Mayhew.
1652.	Nov.	29.	Mris : Barker, wife of Mr. John Barker.
	Dec.	13.	Richard Bailey.
1653.	Sept.	9.	Robert Sparke.
1654.	June	29.	ffrances Goodchild.

1654.	Oct.	3.	Mary Waterhouse.
	Oct.	8.	John Strutton.
	Oct.	26.	John Waterhouse.
1655.	July	11.	Elizabeth Eliot.
1656.	May	3.	Susan ffirmin.
	Aug.	1.	Thomas Merton.
	Feb.	20.	Henry Evat.
1657.	Jan	3.	ffrancis sonne of Arthur Goodchild.
	Jan.	8.	John Brooke.
1658.	May	19.	ffrancis Barret.
	Nov.	5.	Eleanor Loker.
1659.	April	11.	Jeffrey Matthews.
	Nov.	23.	Mris. Keziah Terrill.
1660.	Oct.	3.	Sir William Hervey, Knight.
	Nov.	30.	ffrancis Mourde.
1661.	Feb.	2.	Joseph Mayhu.
1662.	Nov.	12.	James Reinolds.
1663. (?)	May	16.	Ann Johnson.
1663.	June	15.	William Hervey.
1664.	April	21.	Mary Evat.
1665.	June	7.	John Loker sonne of John Loker, Clerk.
	June	16.	Mary Loker daughter of the same.
	June	17.	James Loker sonne of the same.
	June	23.	Margaret Loker daughter of the same.
	July	9.	Agnes daughter of ffrancis Evat.
	July	14.	Richard sonne of Edward Baithorne.
	Aug.	7.	ffrancis Evat.
	Oct.	26.	Thomas Smith.
	Dec.	4.	Mary Smith.
1667.	May	31.	Rose Eliot.
	Sept.	3.	Widow Goldsmith.
	Sept.	24	Jane Barret.

G

1670.	Jan.	12.	William sonne of John Mayhu.
1671.	Oct.	13.	Audrie wife of Robert Day.
1672.	Feb.	5.	Mary Hamond, widow.
1673.	July	31.	John Summers.
	Feb.	20.	Mris. Elizabeth Hervey.
1674.	March	27.	Mother Miles.
1675.	July	18.	John Loker, Rector of Ickworth.
	Dec.	20.	Mr. William Reinolds.
	Jan.	13.	Susan Goodchild.
	Jan.	27.	Bridget Summers, widow.
1676.	Aug.	19.	Edward Baithorne.
1678.	Oct.	11.	Dorothy wife of Walter Derisly.
	Oct.	24.	Mary wife of John Turner.
	March	7.	Jeremiah sonne of John Adams.
1679.	July	14.	Mris. Judeth Reinolds.
	July	17.	Margaret Hammond.
	Nov.	16.	Georg Wyerd.
	Jan.	23.	John Hervey Esq.
1680.	June	25.	Anne Baithorne, widow.
1682.	Nov.	4.	John Rounser.
1683.	Feb.	21.	Susan wife of Arthur Goodchild.
1685.	Aug.	8.	Susan wife of Edward Goodchild.
	Sept.	13.	Robert Day.
	Feb.	5.	Thomas Goodchild.
	Feb.	13.	Sarah Heward.
1686.	March	28.	ffrancis ffenton.
	June	7.	The Lady Isabella Hervey, wife of Sir Thomas Hervey.
	Nov.	23.	Thomas sonne of Mr. Robert Reynolds.
	March	8.	Arthur Goodchild.
1687.	May	27.	Abigal Heward.
	Dec.	17.	Thomas sonne of Mr. Robert Reynolds.
1688.	June	9.	Rachel Murton.

1689.	June	20.	Mris. Keziah Porter.
	Dec.	10.	Anne Strutton.
	March	19.	Margaret Wyard.
1690.	May	30.	Elizabeth Nun.
	Aug.	25.	Giles Hammond.
	March	4.	Grace ffrost.
1691.	June	28.	Margaret Hood.
1692.	March	16.	Isabella wife to Mr. John Hervey Esq., and only daughter of ye Honble. Sir Robert Carr, Baronet.
1693.	April	3.	Anne daughter of Mr. Robert Reynolds.
	Jan.	1.	Frances daughter of Joseph & Frances Alexander.
	Jan.	18.	John son of Thomas & Abigail Murton.
1694.	June	1.	The Honble. Sir Thomas Harvey, Knight.
	Jan.	4.	Elizabeth daughter of ye Honble. John Harvey Esq.
	April	7.	Mrs. Keziah Reynolds, wife to Mr. Robert Reynolds.
1695.	Dec.	8.	Frances daughter of Joseph & Frances Alexander.
	Jan.	3.	Thomas Hervey, Gentleman, yonger son of ye Honble. Sir Thomas Hervey, Knight.
1696.	Dec.	15.	George Strutton, widower.
	Jan.	1.	Giles Cole.
	March	24.	Susan, daughter of Mr. Robert Reynolds.
1697.	April	5.	Thomas Firmin.
	July	11.	Arthur Goodchild sen.
1698.	May	8.	Edith Smee.
	June	21.	Elizabeth Hood.
1699.	Nov.	26.	Mary, daughter of Joseph & Frances Alexander.
	Jan.	15.	William Manning.
	Jan.	30.	Judith, daughter of Joseph & Frances Alexander.
1700.	Sept.	22.	Frances, daughter of Joseph & Frances Alexander.
	Feb.	17.	Keziah, daughter of Robert Reynold of St. Edmunds Bury, Gentleman.
1701.	Dec.	13.	John Turner.
1702.	July	5.	Thomas Murton.

1702. Sept. 21. John Lunden.

Dec. 27. William Pain.

1706. Aug.   7. Mr. James Porter Hervey, son of ye Right Honble.
John Lord Hervey, Baron of Ickworth, & ye Right
Honble. Lady Elizabeth his wife.

Aug. 11. Samuel son of Thomas & Christian Ling.

Nov. 16. Elizabeth Tyler.

1707. Nov.   3. Sarah daughter of Joseph & Frances Alexander.

1708. June   4. Humphry son to ye Right Honble. John Lord Hervey,
Baron of Ickworth.

Oct. 24. Elizabeth daughter of Thomas & Christian Ling.

1709. July 25. Jone Spencer, widow.

Oct. 11. John Summer.

1710. May   6. James son of Thomas & Christian Ling.

May 17. Mary daughter of Thomas & Christian Ling.

May 23. Elizabeth daughter of Joseph & Frances Alexander.

July 20. Felton son to ye Right Hon. John Lord Hervey, Baron
of Ickworth.

1711. May 14. Francis son of Joseph & Frances Alexander.

May 24. Sarah wife of Arthur Goodchild.

Oct. 22. John son of Joseph & Frances Alexander.

Nov. 14. Isabella Carr, eldest daughter of ye Right Hon. John
Lord Hervey, Baron of Ickworth, & ye Right Hon.
Lady Isabella his wife, who was daughter to ye Hon.
Sir Robert Carr, Baronet.

Feb. 19. Christian wife of Thomas Ling.

Feb. 27. James son of Thomas & Christian Ling.

1712. April 29. Henrietta, second daughter of ye Right Hon. John Lord
Hervey, Baron of Ickworth, & ye Right Hon. Lady
Elizabeth his wife.

Oct.   8. Mary Yong.

1713. May   7. The Hon. Mr. James son to ye Right Hon. John Lord
Hervey, Baron of Ickworth.

1714.	July	4.	Sarah Summer, widow.
	July	21.	Susan wife of Samuel Norman.
1715.	Jan.	20.	Marget wife of Arthur Goodchild.
1717.	April	2.	William Langly.
	July	11.	John sonn of Thomas & Christian Ling.
1718.	Dec.	25.	Samuel Norman.
1719.	June	2.	Joseph Alexander, Clerk, late Rector of this Parish.
	Nov.	15.	Robart Jackson.
1720.	April	12.	Richard Evered.
1721.	April	25.	Robert Willman.
1722.	April	29.	Thomas son of John & Mary Everet.
	May	6.	John son of John & Mary Everet.
1723.	Oct.	27.	Abigal wife of Thomas Murton.
	Nov.	24.	The Right honarable Lord Harvie.
1724.	April	4.	Hannah wife of William Everet.
	June	20.	William son of William & Hannah Everet.
	Dec.	19.	John son of Thomas & Elizabeth Nun.
1725.	Feb.	7.	John Pool.
	March	6.	Elizabeth wife of Reachard Everet.
1727.	June	6.	Robart son of Richard Everet.
	July	27.	Barbary daughter of Right Honarable Earl of Bristol.
	Sept.	13.	Elizabeth wife of Mr. Mancel and daughter to Right Honarable Earl of Bristol.
1728.	May	3.	William son of Thomas & Elizabeth Nun.
	May	19.	Frances wife of Arthur Goodchild.
	July	11.	Elizabeth wife of Samawall Norman.
	July	23.	Thomas Arbury.
	Sept.	1.	Isaac Marrat.
1729.	May	26.	Sarah wife of Benjamin Summer.
1730.	June	11.	Mary daughter of Robert & Rose Stocking.
	Feb.		William son of ——— Emet.
1731.	July	18.	Thomas Ling.

1731. March 24. Jane Shel.

1732. May   30. James Crosman.

    July   17. The Lady Henrietta Harve.

1733. June   3. Mr. Joseph Alexander.

    Feb.   19. Mary daughter of Henry Everet.

1734/5. Jan.   3. Oliver Paske.

1736. March 24. Mary Everett.

1737. May   15. Louisa daughter of Sir Robert & Lady Louisa Smyth, (an infant from Bury).

    June   2. Elizabeth wife of George Hilder from Cockfield.

    Aug.   22. Lucy daughter of Thomas & Christian Ling of this Parish.

1738. March 30. Mary Claxton.

    Nov.   1. Thomas Murton, widower.

1740. July   21. Arthur Goodchild, widower.

1741. May   9. The Right Hon. the Countess of Bristol.

1742. July   3. Philip son of James & Rose Crick. Affidavit made the same day.

1743. Aug.   12 The Right Hon. John, Lord Hervey, Baron of Ickworth. N.B. No affidavit being returned, a Penalty of five pounds was incurred and paid according to the Act of Parliament made in that behalf.

    Oct.   22. Mr. Edward Day. Affidavit returned the 30th.

1744. Sept.   8. Mrs. Bridget Adams, House-keeper to the Earl of Bristol.

1745. May   14. Mrs. Elizabeth Morris.

    May   21. Frances Ling, widow.

    Sept. 12. Rebecca daughter of Henry & Sarah Everard.

    Oct.   18. Benjamin Summers.

    Nov.   10. Mary infant base-born daughter of Elizabeth Everard.

1748. Feb.   11. Mrs. Frances Alexander, widow of the Rev. Mr. Alexander.

    Feb.   15. Rebecca wife of John Bladen.

1749. June   3.   Mary daughter of Robert & Rose Stockin. Aff: returned.

      July   22.   Susanna wife of William Emet. Aff: returned.

1750/1 Jan.   27.   The Right Honourable John, Earl of Bristol. No affidavit being returned, a penalty was incurred & paid according to Act of Parliament.

1752. Nov.   14.   William Emmet sen. Aff: returned November 18.

1757. Feb.   3.   Theophilus Wickston. Aff: returned February 7.

1758. June   4.   John Everett.

      Sept.   3.   Thomas son of Joseph & Susanna Prick.

      Nov.   3.   Jane Tuor, widow.

1759. May   10.   William son of Joseph & Susanna Prick.

      July   23.   Sarah wife of Henry Everard.

      July   30.   Richard Moody.

1760. Aug.   9.   Rose daughter of John & Rose Everett.

      Sept.   28.   Rose wife of Robert Stockin.

      Nov.   17.   Anne daughter of Robert & Elizabeth Bridges.

1761. Sept.   18.   Henry Evered.

1762. March 21.   Ann Emmet, an infant.

      Oct.   3.   Richard Williams.

1763. May   15.   Ann Emmet, an infant.

1764. Nov.   20.   William son of William & Mary Emmett.

1765. June   8.   Robert son of Robert & Martha Stocking.

      Aug.   5.   Rose Holden of Horringer.

1767. Oct.   30.   Robert Stocking sen.

1768. Jan.   24.   Mary Wynch.

      Sept.   9.   The Right Hon. Mary Lady Hervey.

1770. April   21.   Mary Boreham.

1771. Feb.   17.   Elizabeth daughter of John & Rose Everett.

      March 17.   Rose daughter of Robert & Martha Stocking.

      May   8.   Henry Everett.

      May   24.   Micah Boreham, an infant.

1771. July   20. The Right Hon. Lady Ann Hervey.
1772. Nov.   2. Rose daughter of Robert & Martha Stocking.
1773. April   27. Mary Everett, widow.
       Aug.   23. The Hon. Mr. Felton Hervey. Mem : The Hon. Mrs.
                     Hervey, his wife, was removed from Bury at the same
                     time, and laid in the same vault.
       Nov.   16. John Everett.
1775. Jan.   24. Mrs. Alexander.
       March   26. The Right Hon. George William, Earl of Bristol.
       Sept.   12. Thomas Bulbrook.
1776. May   1. Mary daughter of John & Mary Wynch.
1779. Dec.   28. Augustus John, Earl of Bristol.
1781. April   1. John Bladen.
1782. April   3. Joseph Prick.
1783. March   28. Hon. & Rev. Dr. Charles Hervey, formerly Rector of
                     this Parish.
1784. Nov.   13. Rose wife of James Crick (late Rose Harsten) aged 72.
1785. Jan.   2. John Winch of Chevington, a married man, aged 66.
       Jan.   15. Mary Ann daughter of Joseph & Elizabeth Prick (late
                     Rasbrook) æt. one year nine months.
1786. March   7. Susanna daughter of Antony & Elizabeth Crick (late
                     Prick) æt. nine weeks.
       Nov.   11. John son of James & Hannah Button.
1787. Jan.   18. John Salter aged 53. (or 63 ?)
1788. Jan.   6. Henry son of Benjamin & Mary Prick.
       March   27. Susannah Prick, widow.
1790. April   18. Benjamin Summers.
1791. Jan.   27. Elizabeth wife of Joseph Prick.
1792. Oct.   20. Elizabeth Summers, widow.
1794. Jan.   10. Hannah wife of James Button (late Petit) aged 44 years.
1795. Feb.   7. Ann daughter of William & Mary Emmett.
       Feb.   22. William Emmett.

1795. May   4. James Button aged 45 years.
      Dec.   31. James Crick aged 90 years.
1796. Sept.   26. John Augustus, Lord Hervey.
1798. Feb.   24. Maria daughter of Ann Sharpe.
1799. June   27. John Frost.
1800. Sept.   11. Mary daughter of Joseph and Sarah Prick (late Cooper).
      Oct.   11. Ann Green.
      Dec.   27. Elizabeth Countess of Bristol.
1802. Nov.   1. Mary Emmett widow, aged 82 years.
1804. April   21. The Right Hon. & Right Rev. Frederick Earl of Bristol, Baron Hervey of Ickworth, and Bishop of Derry in Ireland. Died July 8, 1803, buried April 21, 1804.
      July   1. The Hon. Sophia Amelia Elizabeth Hervey, infant daughter of the Right Hon. Frederick William Hervey, Earl of Bristol, & Elizabeth Albana his wife (late Upton).
      Dec.   27. George Avis, aged 27 years.
1806. Jan.   8. Robert Copsey, Labourer.
1807. Sept.   12. Sarah wife of John Shilitto.
      Nov.   20. Mabel wife of Abraham Steed.
1808. Nov.   26. Jane wife of Michael Thomas Becher.
1810. May   9. Martha Stocking aged 80 years.
      June   25. William Rolfe an infant.
1809. June   28. Mary wife of Benjamin Pryke from Horringer, aged 54.
      July   25. Thomas Midders.
1813. Jan.   2. Henry Cator of Chevington, aged 2 months.
1815. Jan.   29. The Hon. General William Hervey, of London, 82 years.
      May   4. Samuel Glanville, of Ickworth, 71 years.
      May   4. Sarah Green, of Horringer, 9 years.
      July   21. Anne Lennard, of Ickworth, 11 weeks.
1816. Feb.   9. David Lennard, of Ickworth, 2 years.
      April   26. Mary Anne Anderson, of Ickworth, 6 months.

H

1816.	May	9.	Anne Lennard, of Ickworth, 35 years.
	June	6.	Jane Shillito, of Barrow, 13 weeks.
1817.	July	28.	Abraham Steed, of Horringer, 81 years.
1818.	March	17.	Sarah Pryke, of Ickworth, 49 years.
1819.	June	22.	Elizabeth Aves, of Ickworth, 71 years.
1820.	Jan.	16.	Elizabeth Girt, of Ickworth, 36 years.
	Feb.	1.	Joseph Pryke, of Ickworth, 77 years.
	March	19.	Arthur Cross, of Ickworth, 3 weeks.
	Dec.	21.	Ann Button, of Ickworth, 74 years.
1821.	Jan.	4.	Rose Pryke, of Ickworth, 9 years.
	Feb.	10.	Thomas Anderson, of Ickworth, 8 years.
1822.	Jan.	17.	George Shepherd Bilson, of Ickworth, 17 weeks.
	July	21.	Maria Winch, of Ickworth, 13 weeks.
1823.	June	22.	Mary Lennard, of Horringer, infant.
	July	9.	George Cator, of Chevington, 8 years.
1824.	June	13.	Eliza Winch, of Horringer, 12 weeks.
	Dec.	23.	Lucy Howe, of Ickworth, 58 years.
1825.	Dec.	7.	Mary Arborn, of Ickworth, 45 years.
1826.	Feb.	3.	Anne Plumb, of Ickworth, 5 weeks.
	May	18.	Sarah Winch, of Horringer, 14 years.
	July	23.	Mary Cater, of Chevington, 18 weeks.
	Oct.	26.	Henry Howe, of Ickworth, 17 years.
1827.	June	7.	John Shillito, of Barrow, 82 years.
	Dec.	9.	Thomas Winch, of Ickworth, 20 weeks.
1828.	Feb.	28.	Abraham Arborn, of Martins Green, Chevington, 54 years.
	March	8.	Robert Winch, of Horringer, 30 years.
	April	27.	Elizabeth Ann Byford, of Chedburgh, 10 months.
	May	15.	Emily Cross, of Chevington, 18 years.
	Nov.	16.	Sarah, wife of Benjamin Pryke, of Horringer, 53 years.
1829.	Sept.	22.	Thomas Aves, of Ickworth, 77 years.
	Sept.	27.	William Green, of Saxham Parva, 52 years.
	Dec.	1.	Elizabeth Cater, of Chevington, 49 years.

1830. April 14. Ann Winch, of Ickworth, 4 months.

Oct. 7. The Hon. Eliza Harriet Ellis, daughter of the Right Hon. Charles Augustus Ellis, Lord Howard de Walden, of Ickworth. Born Aug. 19, 1829.

1831. Feb. 25. Mary Cross, of Ickworth, 44 years.

1832. June 3. Elizabeth Winch, of Ickworth, 38 years.

Oct. 5. Lady Adelaide daughter of the Right Hon. Frederick William, Earl Jermyn, & the Lady Katharine Isabella, of Ickworth, 7 months.

1834. Jan. 14. Elizabeth Hammond, of Horringer, 14 years.

1835. Oct. 15. Edward John Crack, of Ickworth, 10 years.

Oct. 17. Sarah Crack, of Ickworth, 3 years.

1838. Jan. 15. William Arburn, of Ickworth, 25 years.

April 12. Lord George Hervey, of Ickworth, 35 years. He was buried at Pau in France on Feb. 6, 1838. His remains were deposited in the vault of this Church April 12, 1838.

April 19. Thomas Cross, of Chevington, 6 months.

May 15. Mary Winch, of Horringer, 44 years.

Oct. 24. Mary Everett, of Chedburgh, 33 years.

1839. Jan. 26. Anne, daughter of James & Sarah Arborn, 5 years.

May 10. Harriett Cross Clary, of Ickworth, 12 years.

1840. Feb. 3. Lady Katharine Isabella Hervey, daughter of Earl & Lady Katharine Jermyn, of St. James Parish, London, 16 hours.

June 17. Jane Green, of Horringer, 25 years.

Dec. 21. William Everitt, of Thingoe Union House, of Chevington, 6 years.

1841. March 2. Maria Green, of Horringer, 2 years.

1842. June 19. Mary Emmet, of Chevington, 77 years.

1843. April 25. Sarah Shillito, of Barrow, 32 years,

Sept. 23. Elizabeth Arborn, of Ickworth, 29 years.

1844.	June	5.	Elizabeth Albana, Marchioness of Bristol, 68 years.
	Sept.	9.	Benjamin Pryke, of Horringer, 86 years.
1845.	July	5.	Stephen Shillito, of Barrow, 61 years.
	July	23.	William Anderson, of Ickworth, 76 years.
1846.	March	5.	William Emmett, of Horringer, about 80 years.
1847.	March	24.	James Cross, of Chevington, 65 years.
	Sept.	9.	Sarah Crack, of Ickworth, 47 years.
	Oct.	11.	William Junnicliff, of Ickworth, 16 years.
1848.	Feb.	12.	Sarah Arbon, of Chevington, 38 years.
	April	28.	The Lady Katharine Jermyn, of Ickworth, 39 years.
	April	28.	Lady Sophia Elizabeth Hervey, daughter of Earl & Lady Katharine Jermyn, aged 1 day. Born in Eaton Place, London.
	July	2.	Frances Cross, of Martin's Green, on the borders of Ickworth and Chevington, 42 years.
	Sept.	12.	Robert Rolfe of Rede, 66 years.
	Oct.	14.	James Arborn, of Chevington, 40 years.
	Oct.	30.	James Howe, of Chevington, 84 years.
	Nov.	11.	Park Howlett, of Ickworth, 22 years.
	Dec.	13.	Thomas Cater, of Ickworth, 32 years.
1849.	March	15.	Elizabeth Smith, of Chevington, 44 years.
	May	4.	Ellen Peachey, of Chevington, 7 months.
1850.	Jan.	28.	Arthur Hervey, of Ickworth, 1 day.
	March	27.	Shadrach Cross, of Chevington, 38 years.
	May	14.	Lord William Hervey, of Paris, 44 years. He died at Torquay, May 6.
	July	24.	James Cross, of Ickworth, 43 years.
	Oct.	17.	John Morris, of Ickworth, 98 years.
1851.	Jan.	16.	Jane Massey, of Ickworth, 53 years.
	Aug.	20.	Mary Hammond, of Horringer, 75 years.
1852.	March	15.	Ann Winch, of Ickworth, Martin's Green, 81 years.
	June	25.	John Hammond, of Horringer, 74 years.

1853. April 22. William Sale, of Ickworth, 83 years.

Oct. 24. John Winch, of Barton, 81 years.

1854. Aug. 4. John Cater, of Ickworth, 72 years.

1855. May 21. Ann Anderson, of Bury St. Edmunds, 79 years.

Nov. 15. Samuel George Adams, of Ickworth, 50 years.

1856. June 7. Lady Elizabeth Frederica Hervey, of Eaton Place, London, 23 years.

1858. Oct. 5. Sarah Sale, of Ickworth, 88 years.

1859. Feb. 24. Frederick William, Marquess of Bristol, 89 years.

July 12. Thomas Lennard, of Horringer, 86 years.

Aug. 16. William George French Rosbrook, of Ickworth, 5 weeks.

1860. Dec. 5. Frederica Mary Lucy Hervey, of Ickworth, 16 months.

1861. Feb. 16. Eliza Augusta Caroline Hervey, of Ickworth, 16 years.

1862. May 16. Mary Ann Leonard, of Horringer, 79 years.

Aug. 5. George Goss, of Ickworth, 36 years.

1863. March 21. Jonathan Race, of Ickworth, 11 months.

Nov. 11. Abraham Evered, of Ickworth, 69 years.

1864. Nov. 5. Frederick William, Marquess of Bristol, 64 years.

Nov. 17. Robert Woolsey, of Ickworth, 58 years.

1865. April 10. William Bilson, of Ickworth, 83 years.

Nov. 18. Charlotte Evered, of Bury St. Edmunds, late of Ickworth, 73 years.

1866. Aug. 13. Isaiah Davis, of Ickworth, 42 years.

1867. March 12. Frederick George Robinson Dadley, of Ickworth, 1 month.

1868 Sept. 9. Charles Augustus, Lord Howard de Walden, Baron Seaford, of the British Legation, Brussels, 69 years.

1869. April 9. John Sharpe, of Ickworth, 4 years.

1871. Jan. 3. William Paine of Ickworth Park, Chevington Parish, 75 years.

May 29. Susan Ely, of Ickworth, 87 years.

Nov. 4. Elizabeth Bilson, of Bury St. Edmunds, 90 years.

1871. Dec.   30. Sarah Cater, of Ickworth Park, Chevington Parish, 8 years.
1872. Jan.   6. Ann Prewer, of Ickworth Park, 78 years.
       Oct.   4. Thomas Ely, of Ickworth Park, 81 years.
1874. April 13. James Copping, of Ickworth, 74 years.
1875. March 20. Herbert Vincent, of Ickworth Park, Chevington Parish, 1 year.
       June   2. Lord Augustus H. C. Hervey, of Tonbridge, 37 years.
1877. Oct.   13. Edgar Race, of Ickworth, 3 months.
1878. May   29. John Smith, of Ickworth, 71 years.
       Aug.   3. Patience Squibbs, of Ickworth, 53 years.
1880. Jan.   7. Lily Dadley, of Ickworth, 13 hours.
       Nov.   23. Maud Mary Dadley, of Ickworth, 5 years.
1881. Sept.   5. Sarah Paine, of Chevington, 71 years.
1882. Feb.   9. James Dadley, of Ickworth, 66 years.
       Nov.   27. Rose Maria Edwards, of Ickworth, 16 years.
       Dec.   12. Nelly Kathleen Cross, of Hargrave, 22 months.
1883. Feb.   3. Arthur Harry Vincent, of Chevington, 16 months.
       June   13. Harriet Cater, of Ickworth Park, Chevington, 52 years.
       July   3. Sarah Cater, of Union House, 59 years.
       Dec.   18. Helen Mawson, of Ickworth, 29 years.
1884. April 18. Mary Ransom, of Ickworth, 82 years.
1887. June   6. Dick Fred Cross, of Chevington, 3 months.
1888. Feb.   21. John Prewer, of Bury St. Edmunds, late of Ickworth, 94 years.
       April   9. Melinda Howlett, of Ickworth, 19 years.
       Nov.   14. John Cater, of Ickworth Park, Chevington, 67 years.
1889. March 30. Christiana Wright, of Ickworth, 89 years.
       Nov.   16. Frederick James Vincent, of Ickworth Park, Chevington, 28 years.
1890. Aug.   26. Henry Cross, of Whepstead, 44 years.
       Nov.   22. John Howlett, of Ickworth, 30 years.

TOMB STONES IN ICKWORTH CHURCHYARD.

The following are the inscriptions on all the tomb stones in Ickworth Churchyard, copied by me in June 1891. My time being short, I left out the words " In memory of" or " Here lies " in every case; and also put the word " died " in the place of some of its longer equivalents. The numbering is of course of my giving. Nos. 1 to 41 are on the North side, Nos. 42 to 49 are on the South side.

NORTH SIDE.

1. William Paine, died Dec. 28, 1870, in his 76th year.
Sarah his wife, died Sept. 1, 1884, in her 72nd year.
2. William Bilson died April 1, 1865, in his 84th year. More than 60 years Park keeper.
Elizabeth his wife, died Oct. 31, 1871, aged 90 years.
3. Abraham Evered, died Nov. 6, 1863, aged 69 years.
4. Thomas Eley, died Sept. 30, 1872, in his 82nd year.
Susan his wife died May 24, 1871, in her 87th year.
5. John Winch died Oct. 19, 1853, aged 81 years.
Ann his wife died March 9, 1852, in her 82nd year.
6. Sarah daughter of John and Ann Winch, died May 14, 1826, aged 14.
Also Maria Susan their daughter who died young.
7. Elizabeth daughter of John and Mary Hammond, who died Jan. 10, 1831, aged 11 years.

> Death has been here and borne away
>   A sister from our side,
> Just in the morning of her day
>   As young as we she died.
> We cannot tell who next may fall
>   Beneath the chastening rod,
> One must be first, but let us all
>   Prepare to meet our God.

8. James Button, died April 29, 1795, aged 45 years.
   Hannah his wife died Jan. 7, 1794, aged 44 years.
   Ann his wife died Dec. 17, 1820, aged 71 years.

9. Hannah daughter of James and Hannah Button, died July 30, 1782,
   aged 18 weeks.
   Also John their son, died 1787, aged 21 weeks.

10. Mary Ransom, died Easter day, 1884, aged 82 years.

11. John Cater, died Nov. 9, 1888, aged 68 years.

> Weep not for me, my children dear,
>   To weep 'tis all in vain :
> Christ is our Hope ; we need not fear :
>   We shall all meet again.

12. Harriet wife of John Cater, died June 9, 1883, aged 52 years.
    Also Sarah their daughter aged 8 years.

> Patient and meek beneath affliction's rod
>   And Why ? Her faith and hopes were fixed on things of God.

13. Sarah daughter of John and Elizabeth Cater, died July 1, 1883, aged
    60 years.

14. Benjamin Summers, died Oct. 15, 1745, aged 63 years.

15. Elizabeth wife of George Hilder, died May 30, 1737, aged 62 years.

> Though her affliction was great,
>   God did her now release,
> And prepare her a place,
>   Whear joys shall not cease.

16. Elizabeth, wife of John Cater, died Nov. 27, 1829, aged 46 years.

> 1. Long time I was with pain oppressed,
>   Which wore my strength away,
>   And made me long for heavenly rest
>   That never shall decay.

Thomas, son of John & Elizabeth Cater, died Dec. 7, 1848, aged 31 years.

> 2. Farewell, dear Friends, lament for me no more,
> I am not dead; only gone a while before.
> Dear friends, may you obtain that precious faith
> To smile in anguish and rejoice in death.

17. John Cater, died July 30, 1851, aged 72 years.
18. Mr. Edward Day, died Oct. 26, 1743, aged 59 years.
19. Robert Winch, died March 3, 1828, aged 30 years.

> Reader, consider well thy latter end,
> And make thy Judge thy Saviour and thy Friend;
> Oh! may we all such happy thoughts retain,
> And live to die, and die to live again.

Elizabeth his wife, died June 24, 1832, in the 37th year of her age.

> The Friend of sinners was her friend;
> Trusting in Him she met her end:
> Nor in the judgment shall she fear.
> There shall her Friend as Judge appear.

20. John Poole, died Feb. 5, 1725. He served the Honble. Mr. John Hervey, elder brother of Sir Thomas, ye said Sir Thomas, & the Earl of Bristol his son, upwards of sixty years.
21. Thomas Aubrey, died July 23, 1728, after having served Mr. Baptist May and in the Hervey family upwards of 50 years.
22. Theophilus Wickson, died Dec. 31, 1756, aged 13 years.
23. Mrs. Bridget Adams, died Sept. 5, 1744, in her 33rd year.
24. Mrs. Elisabeth Morris, died May 12, 1745, after having served the Countess of Bristol near 50 years.
25. Mrs. Rebeccy, the wife of John Bladen, died Feb. 13, 1747/8 in her 45th year, after having served the Earl of Bristol upwards of 20 years.
26. Sarah wife of Henry Everard, died July 21, 1758, aged 63 years.
    [*The rest of the inscription is illegible.*]

I

27. Henry Everard, died May 5, 1771, after serving the Earl of Bristol upwards of 60 years, aged 75 years. [The rest of the inscription is illegible.]

28. Patience, wife of Robert Squibbs, died July 29, 1878, aged 54 years.

> We laid her in the hallowed grave
> With hope in Him who died to save.

29. Rose Maria, youngest daughter of Thomas and Frances Edwards, died Nov. 22, 1882, aged 16 years.

> Not gone from memory, not gone from love,
> But gone to our Father's Home above.

30. James Dadley, died Feb. 4, 1882, aged 66 years.
31. Nelly Mawson, aged 29, died Dec. 15, 1883.
32. Mary Ann, daughter of James and Maria Peachey, died July 26, 1845, aged 18 years.   Also Ellen Elizabeth their daughter, died April 27, 1849, aged 7 months.

> This lovely bud so young and fair,
> Called hence by early doom,
> Just came to show how sweet a flower
> In Paradise would bloom.

33. Elizabeth, wife of James Girt, died Jan. 9, 1820, aged 36 years.

> How vain the tears that flow from you
> Which on my grave supply no dew,
> How vain to weep now I am dead ;
> But hope in heavenly realms I'm fled.
> Weep then no more, your sighs forbear,
> And pray to God to meet me there.

34. Samuel Glanville, died April 29, 1815, aged 71 years. He was for upwards of 40 years a faithful servant in the Earl of Bristol's family.
35. George Aves, died Dec. 22, 1780, aged 27 years.
36. Elizabeth, wife of Thomas Aves, died June 16, 1819, aged 71 years.

37. Thomas Aves, died Sept. 16, 1829, aged 77 years.

A tender parent and a faithful friend.

38. Samuel G. Adams, died Nov. 11, 1855, aged 50 years.

In the midst of life we are in death.

39. Isiah Davis, died Aug. 8, 1866, aged 42 years.

I die in hope of a joyful resurrection.

40. James Copping, died April 9, 1874, aged 74 years.
41. Robert Wolsey, died Nov. 13, 1864, aged 57 years.

SOUTH SIDE.

42. Sarah wife of John Shillito, died Sept. 8, 1807, aged 58 years.
John Shillito, died June 2, 1827, aged 83 years.
Jane the daughter of Stephen & Susanna Shillito, born Feb. 28, 1816, died June 2, 1816.
Sarah daughter of Stephen and Susan Shillito died April 15, 1843, aged 30 years.
Stephen Tymm Shillito, died June 28, 1845, in his 62nd year.
43. Stephen Tymm Shillito, of Barrow Hall in this County, died June 28, 1845, in his 62nd year.
44. Lydia, wife of James Howe, died Dec. 17, 1824, aged 58 years.

Affliction sore long time I bore,
Physicians were in vain,
Till death did please to give me ease,
And freed me of my pain.

45. James Howe, died Oct. 24, 1848, in his 84th year.
46. William Sale, died April 17, 1853, in his 84th year.
Sarah his wife died Sept. 29, 1858, in her 89th year.
47. Jane wife of James Massey, died Jan. 9, 1851, aged 53 years.
48. Sarah, wife of Benjamin Pryke sen., died Nov. 10, 1828, in her 53rd year.

> Here lies interred a valued wife,
> Who strove to lead a virtuous life,
> She did to industry incline,
> And trusted in an arm Divine;
> Husband and friends prepare to stand
> With her in Heaven at God's right hand.

49.   Melinda Howlett of Ickworth, born Feb. 22, 1869, died April 4, 1888.

> Had He asked us, well we know
> We should cry, O spare this blow!
> Yes, with streaming tears should pray,
> Lord, we love her, let her stay.

1.

3.

4.

12.

16.

17.

HERALDIC SHIELDS IN ICKWORTH CHURCH.

MONUMENTAL INSCRIPTIONS IN ICKWORTH CHURCH.

These are all (except Nos. 31 and 32) flat stones. The Hervey Monuments form the pavement of the Chancel. The earlier ones, Nos. 1, 2, 3, 4, 5, 6, are not the original Stones, but are the work of Augustus, Earl of Bristol, 1775—1779. Some of these inscriptions are not easy to get at, and I have availed myself of Mr. J. J. Howard's kind permission to make use of "The Visitation of Suffolk" edited by him, and wherein he has given them. I have also taken the plates of shields from his work.

1. ARMS.—*Hervey impaling Drury.*
   Here lieth the body of Thomas Harvé who died 1477 ; and of Jane his wife daughter and heiress of Henry Drewry of Ickworth.

2. ARMS.—*Hervey impaling Cockett.*

In memory of William Hervè born in 1465, dyed in 1538; and of Joan his wife daughter of John Cocket of Ampton in Suffolk. Both buried in St. Mary's Church at St. Edmundsbury.

3. ARMS.—*Hervey Impaling Or, two chevrons Gules, on a Canton of the second a mullet of the first, Pope.*

Here lyeth the body of John Harvaye born 1487, died 11th July 1556 :
and of Elizabeth his wife, daughter of Henry Pope of Mildenhall.

4. ARMS.—*Hervey impaling Poley.*

Here lyeth buried the body of William Hervey born 1509, died 1592 ;
and of Elizabeth his wife the daughter of John Poley of Boxted,
Suffolk.

5. ARMS.—*Hervey impaling Argent, a fess nebuly, between three crosses
crosslet fitchée Gules, Bocking.*

Here lyeth buried the body of John Hervey, born 1555, died 1630;
and of Frances his wife, the daughter of Edmund Bocking of Bocking,
in Suffolk, who died 1620.

6. ARMS.—*Hervey impaling Jermyn.*

Here lyeth buried the body of Sir William Hervey, born 1585, died 1660; and of Susan his wife, the daughter of Sir Robert Jermyn of Rushbrooke in Suffolk, who died 1637.*

7. Mr. William Hervey sonn of Sir William Hervey, died the 23rd day of September 1642.

8. Mrs. Kezia Tyrell of Gipping and daughter of Sir W. Hervey died 22 Nov. 1659.

9. Elizabeth Hervey daughter of Sir Thomas Hervey and Isabella his wife died 18th Feb. 1673, being 13 years and 5 months.

10. William Reynolds the eldest son of James Reynolds and Judith daughter to Sir William Hervey dyed Dec. 17, 1675.

11. Here lies Judith eldest daughter to Sir William Hervey and a most blessed wife to James Reynolds Esq. She died July 12, 1679.

12. *Arms and crest of Hervey.*

Hic jacet Johannes Hervey Armiger (filius Gulielmi Hervey Equitis Aurati) qui erat a Thesauris Serenissimæ Reginæ Catharinæ, uxoremque duxit Elizabetham filiam unicam et hæredem viri prænobilis

---

* This is one of the modern Stones. The original gravestones of Sir William and of Susan his wife, which are still in the Chancel, bear the following inscriptions. (1) Here lyeth buried Sir William Hervey who dyed the 30th day of Sepr. Ano. Dom. in ye year of our Lord 1660. (2) Here lieth buried Dame Susan Hervey the wife of Sir William Hervey who dyed the 6th day of Feb. Ano. Dom. 1637,

Gulielmi Hervey Baronis de Kidbrook in Comitatu Cantiæ, Obiit xviii. die Jan. An. Dom. MDCLXXIX ætat. suæ lxiv.

> Insignis, pollens, largus, perfectus, abundans,
> Moribus, ingenio, munere, corde, bonis.

13, ARMS.—*Hervey impaling a fess between eight billets, May.*

Here lye the bodyes of Sir Thomas Hervey and Dame Isabella his wife, who were most eminent examples of piety, charity, and conjugal affection. She departed this life the 5th of June 1686 in the 61st year of her age; and he the 27th of May 1694 in the 69th year of his age.

> With every Virtue so divinely bless'd
> That each had made them saints without the rest.

14. Here lyeth the body of Thomas Harvey youngest son of Sir Thomas Hervey and Isabella his wife; died the 29th of December, 1695, in the 27th year of his age.

15. Here lyeth the body of Kezia the wife of Robert Reynolds, daughter of Mrs. Kezia Tyrell, the youngest daughter of Sir William Hervey, of this place. She died the 5th day of April MDCXCIIII, æt. 36.

16. ARMS.—*Hervey impaling Gules, on a Chevron Argent, three estoiles Sable, Carr, surmounted by a baron's coronet,*

18.

20.

21.

23.

25.

HERALDIC SHIELDS IN ICKWORTH CHURCH.

To face page 72.

Here lyeth ye body of **Isabella** ye wife ot John Hervey Esqre, since Lord Hervey, Baron of Ickworth, who was sole daughter and heir of Sir Robert Carr of Sleaford in ye County of Lincoln, Baronet. She departed this life ye 7th of March, 1692, in ye 24 year of her age. Many daughters have done virtuously, but thou excellest them all. Prov. xxxi, 29. Here lyeth also ye body of Elizabeth daughter of ye said Isabella and Lord Hervey, who dyed ye 1st of January, 1694.

17. ARMS *of Hervey in a lozenge.*

Here lyeth the body of ye Honble Mrs. Isabella Carr Hervey eldest daughter of ye Right Honble John, Lord Hervey, & Isabella his first wife, who departed this life ye xi of November 1711 ætatis suæ 22.

> Her life by nicest Christian rules was wrought,
> Mixt with no staine nor shaded with a fault ;
> Whose various virtues in that practice shown
> Have equalled been by few, surpassed by none.

18. ARMS.—*Hervey and Carr quarterly, surmounted by a coronet; supporters on either side; an ounce Sable, besantée, ducally gorged and chained Or; crest, on a wreath an ounce passant proper, besantée, ducally gorged and chained Or, and holding a trefoil slipped in his dexter paw proper ; motto, Je n'oublieray jamais.*

Here lieth ye body of The Hon. Carr Lord Hervey, eldest son of ye Right Honble, John, Earl of Bristol, by Isabella his first wife, who departed this life the 14th of Nov. 1723, in ye 33rd year of his age.

19. Here lyeth interred the Lady Elizabeth wife of the Honble Bussy Mansel, and daughter of John Earl of Bristol, who died the 3rd of Sept. 1727.

> Vive pius : moriere pius : cole sacra colentem :
> Mors gravis a templis in cava busta trahet.

K

Beneath the covering of this little stone
Lie the poor shrunk yet dear remains of one
With merit humble, and with virtue fair,
With knowledge modest, and with wit sincere,
Upright in all the social paths of life,
The friend, the daughter, sister, and the wife !
So just in disposition of her soul,
Nature left reason nothing to control ;
Firm, pious, patient, affable of mind,
Happy in life, and yet in death resigned.
Just in the zenith of those golden days
When the mind ripens ere the form decays,
The hand of Fate untimely cut her thread,
And left the world to weep that virtue fled,
Its pride when living, and its grief when dead.

20. ARMS.—*Hervey in lozenge.*

Here lyeth ye body of the Lady Barbarah Hervey, daughter of John,
Earl of Bristol, and of Elizabeth his wife, who departed this life on
Tuesday the 25th day of July, An. 1727, in the 19th year of her age.
Here also lieth buried the Lady Henrietta Hervey, daughter of John,
Earl of Bristol, by Elizabeth his 2nd wife, who was born Sept. 25,
1716, and dyed July 13, 1732.
Here also lyeth the body of the Right Honourable Lady Ann Hervey,
daughter of John, Earl of Bristol, who died July 15, 1771, in the 64th
year of her age.

21. ARMS.—*Hervey.*

Here lyeth the body of the Right Honble. John, Lord Hervey, Baron of
Ickworth, eldest son of John, Earl of Bristol, by Elizabeth his second
wife.   Summoned to Parliament by writ 1733.   He served King
George the Second for many years in the office of Chamberlain, was
afterwards appointed Lord Privy Seal, a Cabinet Privy Councellor, and

twice one of the Lords Justices of this Kingdom.* He died Aug. 5, 1743. Huic versatile ingenium, sic pariter ad omnia fuit, ut natum ad id unum diceres quodcunque ageret.

22. ARMS.—*Hervey, impaling Felton, surmounted by a coronet ; supporters and motto of Hervey.*

Here lyeth the body of Elizabeth, Countess of Bristol, second wife to John, Earl of Bristol, sole daughter and heir of the Right Honourable Sir Thomas Felton, of Playford Hall in this County, Baronet, Comptroller of the Household to Queen Ann. She died 1st May 1741, in the 65th year of her age.

Mortua obtinuit plurima quæ meruit.

23. ARMS.—*Hervey, bearing two escucheons ; on one the arms of Carr, and on the other the arms of Felton ; surmounted by an Earl's Coronet.*

---

*The Cullum copy of this inscription has, "He was born Oct. ye 15, 1696, and dy'd" &c.

Here lyes the body of the Right Honourable John, Earl of Bristol,
Lord Hervey, Baron of Ickworth, who was born Aug. 27, 1665, and
dyed Jan. 20, 1751.

24. Here lyeth the body of the Right Honble. Mary, Lady Hervey, relict of
John, Lord Hervey, and daughter of Brigadier Lepell, one of the
Maids of Honour to Caroline, Princess of Wales; Born 26 Sept. 1706,*
died 2 Sept. 1768.

> Awhile oh linger, sacred shade !
> Till ev'ry solemn due be paid ;
> The tears from filial love that flow,
> The sighs that friendship long must know !
> But ah ! within this narrow space
> How each engaging virtue trace ?
> How shall each sweetness be defin'd
> That grace thy form, or bless thy mind?
> Charms that in youth attractive shone,
> Glow'd ripe in their meridian sun,
> And spite of ruthless winter's rage,
> Melted into becoming age.
> Knowledge matured the fruits of sense,
> Nor shook the bloom of diffidence ;
> So silent and so modest too,
> As tasting but what others knew.
> Proud of humility, the sage
> In thy unvarying temper's page
> Or saw, or might have deign'd to see
> The beauties of Propriety.
> Nor while sustain'd each decent part
> Could Prudence self pervert thy heart ;
> Through life thy ev'ry friend the same,
> Each foe thy study to reclaim.

---

*The Cullum copy of this inscription has 1700, which is probably right.

Pain could not chase thy friendly smile ;
Not to afflict was all thy toil ;
Thy woes alone unwont to speak,
For Patience dwelt upon thy cheek.
But in the solemn scene of death
How paint the calm of fleeting breath ?
When fortitude resembled ease,
And the last pang seem'd most to please !
In vain the Sculptor or the Muse
So sad, so sweet a theme pursues ;
The chisel drops, th' unfinished strain
Respects the son it sooths in vain.

Hon. Horace Walpole Esq., fecit.

25. ARMS.—*Hervey, impaling a cinquefoil within a bordure engrailed Ermine, Ashley.*

Here lyeth the body of the Honble. Felton Hervey, the 10th son of John Earl of Bristol, who was born the 12th of Feb. 1712, and died the 16th of August 1773 : and of Dorothy his wife, daughter of Solomon Ashley Esqre, born the —— of ———— 1722, and who died the —— of Nov. 1761.

26. Here lieth the body of Thomas the son of Robert and Kezia Reynolds, who died Dec. 15, 1687.

27. Here lieth the body of Thomas Reynolds the son of Robert Reynolds, who dyed Nov. 22, 1686.

28. Here lyeth the body of Susan the daughter of Robert Reynolds and Kezia his wife, who died March 22, 1696, aged 8 years and 7 months.

29. Here lyeth the body of Frances the daughter of Joseph Alexander, Clerk, and Frances his wife, who dyed Dec. 29, 1693, aged 1 year and 9 months. Here lieth another Frances who died Dec. 8, 1695.

30. Here lieth the bodies of three children, the daughters of Joseph Alexander and Frances his wife. The first is Mary who dyed Nov. 24, 1699, being a year old. The second is Judeth who dyed Jan. 30, 1699, •being 3 weeks old. The third is Frances who dyed Sept. 20, 1700, aged 3 years.

31. Nov. 18, 1808. Jane wife of Rev. M. T. Becher, M.A., Master of Bury School.

32. *A white marble stone on the North Wall.*

Janettæ suæ infra positæ vir uxori quod potuit MDCCCVIII. Locum monumenti dedit Henricus Hasted, A.M. C.C, Cantab olim socius, hujus ecclesiæ Rector, idemque quondam vidui cum multa laude discipulus, Michaelis Thomæ Becher A.M. inauspicato defuncti 3tio die Junii 1809, et apud Buriam Sancti Edmundi, ubi per annos 21 Archididascali munere (eoque celeberrime) functus erat, sepulti. (Cui hoc marmor strui, hoc Epitaphium dicari in animo fuit). Voluntatem peregit testamenti sui Curatrix Sophia Stanley. MDCCCIX.

33. *A marble stone over North door.*

In memory of James Copping, born Jan. 2, 1800, died April 9, 1874. Also of Rebecca Copping his sister, born March 12, 1796, died July 5, 1869. To commemorate their worth and long faithful domestic service at Ickworth, his of 52 years, hers of 43 years, this tablet is erected by Frederick William John, Marquis of Bristol.

THE CULLUM NOTES ON ICKWORTH CHURCH.

I am much obliged to Mr. Gery Milner-Gibson-Cullum for sending me a transcript of " Notes on Ickworth Church, Suffolk, by the Rev. Sir John Cullum, 6th Bart, F.R.S. and F.S.A. Taken fully 16th Feb, 1779." These notes have later additions to them in the handwriting of his brother, Sir Thomas Gery Cullum, and are amongst the MSS. at Hardwick House, near Bury St. Edmunds. I print the Cullum notes bodily, only omitting those inscriptions which I have already given. Sir John says : The pavement of the Chancel, which is not a small one, consists entirely of flat stones for the Hervey family; the earliest I can find is thus inscribed : Heere was buried William Harve Esquyer the 2 day of November 1592. (born 1509.)

Here was buried Frances Harve the wife of John Harve Esquyer the 22 day of Februarie 1620. (Her name was Bocking.)

Heere lieth buried the Bodie of John Harve Esquyer 1630. (He was the eldest son of William Harve Esq. and was 75 years old at his death.)

Here lyeth buried Dam Susan Hervey the wife of Sir William Hervey who dyed the 6 day of Feb. Ano Dom. 1637. (She was daughter of Sir Robert Jermyn of Rushbrook.)

Here lyeth buried Sir William Hervey who died 30 day of Sept. Ano Dom. in the year of our Lord 1660. (Born 1585. Son and Heir of the above John Hervey Esq.)*

On a flat stone at W. end of the Church : Hic jacet Josephus Alexander A.M. hujus Ecclesiæ Rector vere Israelita, in quo dolus not erat. Obiit xxx die Maii A.D. 1719, ætatis suæ LXVII.

Johannes filius Josephi Alexander et Franciscæ uxoris obiit Oct. 19 A.D. 1711, ætatis suæ 16. Francesca uxor Josephi Alexander obiit 7 Feb. A.D. 1747 ætat. 84.

At the W. end of Church contiguous to his Father's : Here lieth ye body of Joseph Alexander L.L.B., son of the Rev. Mr. Joseph Alexander (formerly

---

* Here follow Nos. 12, 15, 13, 19, 18, just as I have already printed them. S. H. A. H.

Rector of this Parish) by Frances his wife. He died May 31, 1733, aged 39 years.*

Hatchment in Church. I suppose the late Lord's, who died at Bath 20 March 1775, and was buried here.

Augustus Earl of Bristol died at London 15 Dec. 1779, and was buried in the Dormitory built by himself on 21.

Frederick Earl of Bristol, Bishop of Derry, died at Albano near Rome 8 July 1803, his body was removed from thence to Naples, and put on board a man of war to be conveyed to England in the Month of October, 1803; but it was not put on shore for several months, and was only deposited in the family burying place at Ickworth on 21 April, 1804.

Inscription on the obelisk in Ickworth Park. Sacred to the memory of Frederick Earl of Bristol, Bishop of Derry, who during 35 years that he presided over that see, endeared himself to all denominations of Christians resident in that extensive Diocese. He was the Friend and Protector of them all; his great Patronage was uniformly administered upon the purest and most disinterested principles. Various and important public works were undertaken at his instigation, and completed by his munificence; and hostile sects which had long entertained feelings of deep animosity towards each other were gradually softened and reconciled by his influence and example. Grateful for benefits which they can never forget, the inhabitants of Derry have erected at Ickworth, where his mortal remains are deposited, this durable record of their attachment. The Roman Catholic Bishop and the Dissenting Minister resident at Derry were among those who contributed to this Monument.

The following is the inscription on the opposite pannell of the Pedestal.

Opus hoc concivium benevolentia Patri institutum grato animo accepit et qua par est pietate auxit filius.

---

* Here follow Nos. 6, 1, 4, all of which Sir John calls "Modern", 17, 2, called "Modern—within the rails", 3, "Modern—next the last", 20, "New—within the rails", 25, 22, 16, 21, 24, 23, 32. S.H.A.H.

*After giving the inscription on the tombstone of Mary, Lady Hervey, (No. 24)
and adding a sketch of her character from Lord Chesterfield's 199th letter to his
son, and a notice of her in the dedication to her of Mr. Walpole's " Anecdotes of
Painting in England," the Cullum MS goes on thus :—*The following inscription
on an altar monument forms a strong contrast to the foregoing. Lady
Hervey and honest Ned Day could not differ more widely from one another
in their lives than do their epitaphs in their styles : in which affectation and
refinement on one hand and plainness and simplicity on the other are
probably characteristic of their respective subjects. (In the Churchyard.)
Mr. Edward Day, born not of wealthy but of honest Parents, in the County
of Cambridge, died the 20th of October, 1743, aged 59.   In his younger
years he served the Duke of Kingston : in his latter the Earl of Bristol,
with credit and reputation.   Though plac'd in a station of dependence, he
was not servile or mean : though rais'd above the common rank of servants,
he was not haughty or over-bearing.   Unpractis'd in the arts of flattery or
the guilt of hypocrisy, he spoke the dictates of his heart with an honest
simplicity.   Let others be transmitted to posterity fam'd for their learning,
wealth or brave exploits : to whatever qualification he possess'd he added
real worth and lustre by the single virtue of sincerity.   This invigorated his
respective duties to his Master, his Friends and Relations.   By a prudent
frugality he acquir'd a moderate fortune, which he divided equally among
his relations ; who out of gratitude and respect have erected this monument
to his memory.

This Church belonged to the Abbey of Bury by the gift of Theodred
Bishop of London. [Theodredus the good, Bishop of Elmham, the 25th
Bishop of London, anno 938. See Beatson's Index.] The termination of
his name is twice upon fragments of glass in the E. window, which is very
ancient and strong.   It is somewhat strange that there should not be a
single memorial of the Drury family, from which the Ickworth estate passed
into the Hervey by marriage.

L

On the only bell is this inscription, not antient ;

> Tho : Gardener he did me cast ;
> I'll sing his praise unto the last.

In Preston Churchyard about 2 miles from Brighton : In memory of Lady Emily Caroline Nassau Hervey, daughter of John Lord Hervey of Ickworth, eldest son of John first Earl of Bristol, who was called to the House of Peers during the life time of his father, and appointed Lord Privy Seal to King Geo : II. Her Ladyship died the 4th of June, 1814, in the 80th year of her age.

As the following inscription is somewhat singular and commemorates a Suffolk lady, I insert it in this collection. It is on a flat marble at the E. end of the S. isle of West Ham Church in Essex :—Here lyeth the body of the right honorable Lady Louisa Carolina Isabella Hervey, daughter to John Earl of Bristol, and wife to Sir Robert Smyth of Isfield in the County of Sussex Bart, who after 38 years marriage died May XI, 1770, aged 55.

> A matron equal to all stations,
> Worthy of the highest, content with the humblest.
> In Beauty an ornament even to her Race ;
> In Œconomy an example to her sex ;
> In Benevolence an honour to her species.
>
> Stay, wretched husband, stop thy heedless hand ;
> Cease stars to count, cease numbering the sand ;
> Whither, o whither would thy frantic grief !
> From mortal praise tis vain to seek relief :
> Vain the long roll of virtues to display ;
> Thy votive brass and marble shall decay.
> The sacred trust to nought material's given ;
> Her virtues record and reward's in Heaven.

[This is the end of the Cullum MS so far as Ickworth is concerned.— S.H.A.H.]

DEEDS RELATING TO ICKWORTH PARSONAGE.*

1. *A terrier of the glebes belonging to the Parsonage of Ickworth, Sept.* 4, 1707.

Imprimis. A Parsonage house containing formerly an Hall, a parlour, a dayry & buttery, two little lower chambers & three upper chambers, but now burnt down.

Item one barn & one stable.

Item five acres of pasture grounds lying round about the parsonage house.

Item one rood of ground lying in Ickworth great common field, abutting on the south upon a wood called the Lown wood; upon the north upon the foot path from Chevington; upon the east upon the ground of Thomas Troughton of Chevington, now John Frost's late of Ickworth.

Item one acre of land lying in Prime Field within the bounds of Chevington, abutting on the east upon a piece of glebe land belonging to the Parsonage of Chevington; on the north upon the High-way.

An Inventory of the goods of the Church.

Imprimis. One Great Bible. A book of Common Prayer, with the articles & canons, and the book of Homilys & a Register.

Item a surplice and Hood, a communion-table, Table-cloth, carpet and napkin.

Item a Pewter flagon, a silver cup & a silver plate.

Exhibited at ye Bishop of Norwitch visitation in ye year 1706. Joseph Alexander, Rector of Ickworth.

2. *A copy of a Terrier of ye glebe lands belonging to ye Parish of Ickworth dated June 20th,* 1716, *with extracts from two others.*

Imprimis. Five acres of Pasture Ground lying round about ye par-

* I find the four following deeds among some papers belonging to my father.—S.H.A.H.

sonage barn, which is yet standing & is under ye care of ye Right
Honble John Earl of Bristol by agreement between him ye said Earl of
Bristol & Joseph Alexander present Incumbent, with ye consent of ye
Right Rev. Father in God' Charles present Bishop of Norwitch, as
appears by an instrument for that purpose bearing date July 23, 1712.

Item one rood of ground lying in Ickworth common Field, abutting on
ye South upon a wood called ye Lown wood, & on ye North upon ye
foot-path from Chevington, & on ye East upon ye ground formerly of
Thomas Troughton & since of John Frost of Ickworth aforesaid.

Item one acre of land lying in Primefield within ye bounds of Chevington, abutting on ye East upon a piece of glebe land belonging to ye
parsonage of Chevington, & on ye North upon ye highway.

As for ye Parsonage house of Ickworth aforesaid, ye Right Honble
Earl of Ickworth (sic) aforesaid Patron of ye said living of Ickworth,
upon ye unhappy accident of its being burnt down by fire, considering
ye smallness of ye said living together with ye present Bishop of ye
Diocess have thought fit to unite ye said living of Ickworth to another
living called Chedburgh because of their nearness to one another, and
have further consented that there should be no more parsonage house
in Ickworth aforesaid, as appears by a faculty for that purpose from ye
Right Revd. Bishop aforesaid bearing date Feb. 2, 1712.

Memorandum. Both ye Tith & Glebe are leased out to ye Right
Honble Earl of Bristol aforesaid for forty pounds yearly to ye present
Incumbent etc, as appears by ye instrument for that purpose bearing
date as aforesaid, July 23, 1712.

Joseph Alexander, Rector of Ickworth.

Benjamin Summer, only Churchwarden.

*An Inventory of ye goods & utensils belonging to ye Church of Ickworth
aforesaid.*

Imprimis. A Bible, also a Book of Common prayer, articles & Homilys.

Item a surplice & hood.

Item a scarlet cloth for ye Communion Table, a pewter flagon, a silver cup & patin, also a linnen cloth & napkin.

Item a Green cloth for ye pulpit &' cushin & ye Desk lined with the same.

Item one large Bell.

Joseph Alexander, Rector of Ickworth.
Benjamin Summer, only Churchwarden.

Extract from Terrier dated June 28, 1740.

All tithes belonging to the Parish of Ickworth are paid to the Earl of Bristol in their proper kinds, and he allows forty pound a year to the Rector for the whole tithes.

Charles Hervey, Rector.

Extract from Terrier dated May 30, 1791.

Memorandum. All Tythes belonging to the Parish of Ickworth aforesaid are paid to the Earl of Bristol in their proper kinds, and he allows forty pounds a year to the Rector in lieu of the tythes and Glebe lands.

Thomas Knowles, Rector of Ickworth,
James Button, Churchwarden.

3. *A faculty from ye Bishop of Norwitch to make use of ye materials remaining of Ickworth Parsonage in ye repairs of Chedburgh, and an exemption from Ickworth dilapidations.*

Charles by divine permission Lord Bishop of Norwich to our well beloved in Christ Joseph Alexander, Clerk, Rector of the parishes and parish Churches of Ickworth and Chedburgh in the County of Suffolk and Dioces of Norwich, health in our Lord. Whereas we have lately received a petition under the hand of you the said Joseph Alexander, shewing unto us that the Parsonage house of Ickworth aforesaid being at your first coming into that benefice (which is about twenty years since) was in great decay and not habitable, and nothing was or could be recovered from the widow of your predecessor, she being left in mean circumstance, was by you pulled down and rebuilt at above seven score pounds charge, that the said house.was unfortunately burnt down by an accidentall fire about ten years since, only some pieces of timber being saved, and that there is a Parsonage house at Chedburgh aforesaid, (which said Rectories of Ickworth and Chedburgh are both at the presentation of the Right Honorable John Lord Hervey, true and undoubted patron of the same, and designed by his Lordship to be by succeeding Rectors held united,) which with some charge may be made convenient for the habitation of the Rector of both parishes and his family, and that the said parishes are but smal and very near contiguous ; and the profitts of both Rectories united but a bare competency for one Minister, and two houses rather a burden than of any use to the succeeding Rectors, wherein you humbly prayes our license and faculty to discharge you and your heirs from all ruins and dilapidations of the said Parsonage house of Ickworth, and to make use of the remaining materials in and about the repairing and adorning the Parsonage house and outhouses of Chedburgh aforesaid, which will cost thirty pounds ; Being certified of the truth and reasonablenes of your said petition under the hands of divers neighbouring clergymen and gentlemen, who by virtue of our commission of inspection to them directed did view and inspect the same, and haveing received the consent of the said Right Honorable John Lord Hervey, the true and undoubted patron of both the said Parish Churches, as in and by your said petition and certificate and patron's consent filed in our principal Registry may more at large appear ; That in consideration of the premises we the said Bishop of Norwich by vertue of our power and authority ordinary and episcopal do hereby (as far as by law we may) by this our license and faculty to you the said Joseph Alexander given and granted exonerate and discharge you and your successors, Rectors of the said parish and parish Church of Ickworth aforesaid, from the rebuilding the said Parsonage house of Ickworth or any part thereof; and do also hereby impower you the said Joseph Alexander to apply the remaining materials of the said Parsonage house of Ickworth toward the repairing the said Parsonage house of Chedburgh, enjoyning you also to lay out thirty pounds or whatever sum shall be needfull to put the said Parsonage house of Chedburgh in good repair and make it convenient for the habitation of the Rectors of both the aforesaid parishes and their families according to the tenor of your said petition ; And to certifie us or our Vicar General what you have done in the premises, (particularly what is the value of the said remaining materials of the said Parsonage house of Ickworth aforesaid, and how you have disposed of the same, and what money you have laid out in and about the repairing the said Parsonage house of Chedburgh aforesaid,) at or before the twenty ninth day of September next ensuing. Given under our episcopall seal the second day of February, in the year of our Lord Christ, one thousand, seven hundred and twelve, and of our consecration the fiith.

C. NORWICH.

4. *The union of Ickworth & Chedburgh.*

Carolus permissione divina Norvicensis Episcopus dilecto nobis in Christo Josepho Alexander, Clerico, A.M. Rectori ecclesiæ parochialis de Ickworth in Com : Suffolciæ, necnon Rectori ecclesiæ parochialis de Chedburgh in comitatu prædicto nostrarum Norvicensis dioces : et jurisdictionis, salutem. Cum, ut informamur, Rectoriæ ecclesiæ parochialis de Ickworth fructus, redditus, proventus, decimæ et emolumenta ecclesiæ tenues et exiles sunt, cumque etiam Rectoriæ ecclesiæ parochialis de Chedburgh fructus, redditus, proventus, decimæ et emolumenta ecclesiæ adeo tenues et exiles sunt ut ad congruam sustentationem

Rectoris ibidem pro tempore existente juxta clericalis ordinis decentiam et aliorum onerum eidem incumbenti supportationem minime sufficiant, nec sufficere potuerint in futurum, propter igitur tenuitatem et exiguitatem eorumdem beneficiorum et alias causas coram nobis præpositas ac per nos previo examine approbatas; præfatam Rectoriam de Chedburgh cum suis juribus, membris et pertinentiis universis præfatæ Rectoriæ de Chedburgh durante tuâ incumbentiâ in eâdem Rectoriâ de Chedburgh, et quamdiu fueris Rector ibidem et non aliter autoritate nostrâ ordinariâ quatenus in nobis est jura et statuta hujus inclyti regni Angliæ patiuntur et non aliter, neque alio modo unimus, annectimus et incorporamus per præsentes, ita quod tu præfatam Rectoriam de Ickworth una cum dictâ Rectoriâ de Chedburgh unius tantummodo beneficii nomine quamdiu fueris Rector ejusdem Rectoriæ de Ickworth retinere, fructusque redditus et proventus utriusque beneficii (debitis et congruis eorumdem supportatis oneribus) recipere in tuos usus et utilitatem convertere et applicare, libere et licite possis et valeas (contrariis ordinationibus ecclesiasticis non obstantibus) : proviso nihilominus quod idoneum curatum habeas et constituas autoritate nostrâ ordinariâ licentiandum et probandum, qui plebem ejusdem parochiæ in quâ non residebis instruat et informet, si facultates ejusdem beneficii talem curatum sustinere commode nobis videbitur. In aujus rei testimonium sigillum nostrum episcopale præsentibus apponi fecimus. Datum septimo die mensis Augusti, anno Domini millimo septuingimo duodecimo, nostræque consecrationis quinto.   C. Norvicen.

RECTORS OF ICKWORTH.

I take the following list of the Rectors of Ickworth from Gage's History of Thingoe Hundred, published in 1838.

2 Non. Maii 1307.	Walt. fil. Dni. Jois de Gedding, ad præs. Thomæ de Ikeworth.
3 Kal. Julii 1335.	Sim. de Saxham, ad præs. ejusdem.
15 Aug.	Walt. Shortwode de W. Bradenham, ad præs. Thomæ de Ikeworth.
22 Jan. 1380.	Joes Chabrok, ad præs. Thomæ de Ikworth.
20 Sept. 1403.	Joes Woringaye de Wysbech, ad præs. Joes Cokerell de Orford.
10 Julii 1412.	Galf. Shavere de Thuxton (per mut. cum S. Mich. Fyncham ad præs. Isabellæ com. Suff. Katerinæ relictæ Jois Cokerell etc.
22 Julii 1424.	Mr. Rob. Braunche alias Derham (per mut. cum Brynton) ad præs. Kat. Cokerell mulieris.
12 Dec. 1426.	Rob. Sherman (per mut. cum Sudbur. Omn. Sanct.) ad præs. Will. Drury mil. etc.
5 Martii 1449.	Tho. Brynnyngr alias Sheder, ad præs. Humfr. Ducis Buckingham.
9 Sept. 1477.	Mag. Rob. Paman, ad præs. Willi. Carew, arm.
13 Apr. 1503.	Will. Giles, ad præs. Willi. Hervey, arm.
19 Martii 1528.	Will. Hervey (æt. 17), ad præs. Jois Hervey, arm.
4 Junii 1542.	Joes Barret, ad præs. ejusdem. Joes Buckenham.
11 Dec. 1595.	Will. Withers, ad præs. Jois Hervey, arm.
3 Junii 1614.	Will. Welles, ad præs. Will. Hervey, mil.

M

14 Junii 1636.	Will. Sudbury, ad præs. ejusdem.
	Joes Lockyer.
13 Aug. 1675.	Abraham Underwood, ad præs. Jois Hervey, arm.
6 Dec. 1692.	Joseph Alexander, ad præs. Thomæ Hervey, mil.
10 Nov. 1719.	Rob. Butts, ad præs. Jois Com. Bristol.
6 Aug. 1736.	Honorabilis vir Carolus Hervey, ad præs. ejusdem.
10 Jan. 1748.	Thomas Knowles, ad præs. ejusdem.
30 Martii 1803.	Henricus Hasted, ad præs. Fred. Will. Com. Bristol.
16 Nov. 1832.	Dominus Arthur Hervey, per resig. Henrici Hasted, ad præs. Fred. Will. March. Bristol.

I presume that some deficiency in the Episcopal Registers at Norwich prevented Mr. Gage from giving the date of the termination of the incumbencies of John Barret and William Sudbury, and the date of the incomings of their respective successors, John Buckenham and John Lockyer, or Loker as he is always called in the Ickworth Registers. Possibly the Ickworth Registers may supply those missing dates, a John Barret being buried in 1566, and a William Sudbury in 1644. The name Paman will be found in the Registers long after the Rector of that name had departed, and the Buckenhams also lingered on awhile after the coming of another Rector. One wonders where they lived, and what they did.

Robert Butts was son of William Butts, Rector of Hartest in Suffolk; he was educated at Bury Grammar School and Trinity College, Cambridge; Rector of Ickworth 1719; Dean of Norwich in 1731, Bishop of Norwich in 1733, translated to Ely in 1738, and died at Ely House, Holborn, in 1748. Several letters to him will be found in the Letter-books of John, Lord Bristol, who seems to have had a very sincere regard for him.

Charles Hervey was 5th son of John, 1st Earl of Bristol; born in 1703, educated at Queen's College, Cambridge, Rector of Ickworth and afterwards of Sproughton and Shotley; made a Prebendary of Ely in 1742, and died there in 1783.

Thomas Knowles is said by Allibone to have been a native of Ely and Fellow of Pembroke Hall, Cambridge. He was the author of some religious works. He was buried in Chedburgh Church, where there is a stone with this inscription : In memory of the Rev. Thomas Knowles D.D. Rector of Ickworth and Chedburgh, Prebendary of Ely, and Preacher of St. Mary's Church, Bury, who died Oct. 6, 1802, aged 78 years.

Henry Hasted was born at Bury St. Edmunds in 1771 ; educated at the Bury Grammar School and Christ's College, Cambridge ; 6th wrangler in 1793 ; Preacher or Lecturer at St. Mary's, Bury, from 1802 to 1842 ; Rector of Ickworth and Chedburgh from 1803 to 1832, and Rector of Horringer from 1814 to his death in 1852, aged 81 years.

Arthur Charles Hervey, 4th son of Frederick William, 1st Marquis of Bristol, was born on Aug 20, 1808 ; educated at Eton and Trinity College, Cambridge, going out in the first class of the classical Tripos of 1830 ; appointed to the Rectory of Ickworth cum Chedburgh in 1832 ; in 1852 Chedburgh was separated from Ickworth, and Horningsheath or Horringer united to it instead, which two livings (Ickworth and Horringer) he held till 1869 ; appointed Archdeacon of Sudbury in 1862, and Bishop of Bath and Wells in 1869. Whilst these pages are passing through the press his long, active and useful life, active and useful to the very last, has reached its end. He died after a very short illness while on a visit at Hackwood House, near Basingstoke, on Saturday, June 9, 1894, aged 85 years, and was buried at Wells Cathedral on June 14. He was a contributor to Dr. Smith's Dictionary of the Bible, and to the Speaker's Commentary, and was also a member of the Old Testament Revision Company. He published two volumes of Parochial Sermons in 1850; a volume on the Genealogies of our Lord in 1853 ; and a volume of Sermons on the Inspiration of Holy

Scripture (preached before the University of Cambridge in 1855) in 1856, besides single sermons, charges, lectures, etc.

It is, perhaps, worth noting that Lord Arthur Hervey and his two immediate predecessors together held the Rectory of Ickworth for 121 years, and might have held it (if Lord Arthur had not been promoted) for 146 years. Mr. Knowles, appointed by the first Lord Bristol who was born early in the reign of Charles II, held it for 55 years ; Mr. Hasted succeeding him held it for 29 years, and might have held it for 49 years ; Lord Arthur Hervey succeeding him held it for 37 years, and might have held it for 61 years.

On the promotion of Lord Arthur Hervey to the See of Bath and Wells in the latter part of 1869, the Rev. Dr. Burgess, Rector of Upper Chelsea, was appointed to the Rectory of Ickworth and Horringer.

At his death in 1881, the Rev. Arthur Linzee Chatterton Heigham was appointed.

At his resignation in 1883, the present Rector, the Rev. James Giddens, was appointed.

THE POPULATION.

The census returns for 1801 give Ickworth 7 inhabited houses, occupied by 11 families ; 36 males, 31 females ; 15 persons chiefly employed in Agriculture, 9 in Trade, Manufactures or Handicraft, 43 all others ; Total 67.

The returns for 1811 give 12 inhabited houses, occupied by 13 families ; 8 families chiefly employed in Agriculture ; 1 in Trade, Manufactures or Handicraft ; 4 all others ; 26 males, 42 females ; Total 68.

The returns for 1821 give 14 inhabited houses, occupied by 14 families, 36 males, 46 females ; Total 82.

The returns for 1831 give Ickworth 1350 acres; 7 inhabited houses, occupied by 10 families, 1 uninhabited* house; 3 families chiefly employed in Agriculture, o in Trade &c., 7 all others; 19 males, 24 females; Total 43.

The returns for 1841 give 1350 acres; 12 inhabited houses, 1 uninhabited; 31 males, 31 females; Total 62.—Of these 62, 49 are set down as born in the County, and 13 elsewhere: 12 males and 10 females under 20; 19 males and 21 females over 20.

The returns for 1851 and 1861 I could not find in the British Museum.

The returns for 1871 give 1259 acres; 12 inhabited houses; 50 males, 65 females; Total 115.

The returns for 1881 give 13 inhabited houses, occupied by 13 families, 1 uninhabited† house; 44 males, 51 females; Total 95.

Ickworth is a discharged Rectory, valued in the King's books at £7..11..5½

The money raised by the Parish Rates in 1803 was £92..1..6½, at 3s. 4d. in the pound.

---

* Probably the big house, which being empty would account for the considerable decrease in the population.—S.H.A.H.

† This would be Ickworth Lodge, which being empty would answer for a diminution in the population of about 20.

INDEX.

BAPTISMS, MARRIAGES, AND BURIALS.

BAPTISMS.

ADAMS Amy 1587.
— Jeremiah 1678.
— John 1581.
— Lidia 1680.
— Ralf 1583.
ALBON ⎱ Abraham 1830.
ARBORN ⎰ Ann 1809, 1834.
— Annies 1849.
— Elizabeth 1814.
— Emma 1836.
— Harriet 1827.
— James 1808, 1845.
— Jane 1816.
— Jane Anna 1847.
— Susan 1824.
— Thomas 1818.
— William 1811, 1829, 1838.
ALEXANDER Frances 1695, 1697.
— Francis 1711.
— John 1694.
— Joseph 1693.
— Judith 1700.
— Marget 1702.
— Mary 1698.
— Sarah 1707.
— William 1701.
ANDERSON Mary Ann 1815.
— Sarah Ann 1824.
AVES ⎱ Augustus 1784.
ALVIS ⎰ John 1782.
— Joseph 1806.
— Marianne 1825.
— Robert 1808.
— William 1787.

MARRIAGES.

ABBOT Henry 1681.
— John 1705.
ADAMS Alice 1692.
— Roger 1802.
— William 1658.
ALBON John 1822.
ALEXANDER Ann 1696.
— Joseph 1695.
ALINGTON William 1570.
ALLWINKLE Isaac 1696.
AMES Christian 1695.
ANDERSON Sarah 1835.
AVIS Sophia 1802.
— Thomas 1638, 1821.

BURIALS.

ABBOT Ede 1593.
ABELL Mary 1590.
ADAMS Bridget 1744.
— Jeremiah 1678.
— Samuel George 1855.
ALEXANDER Elizabeth 1710.
— Frances 1693, 1695, 1700, 1748.
— Francis 1711.
— John 1711.
— Joseph 1719, 1733.
— Judith 1699.
— Mary 1699.
— Mrs. 1775.
— Sarah 1707.
ALLINGTON Mary 1626.
ANDERSON Ann 1855.
— Mary Ann 1816.
— Thomas 1821.
— William 1845.
ARBURY Thomas 1728.
ARBORN Abraham 1828.
— Ann 1839.
— Elizabeth 1843.
— James 1848.
— Mary 1825.
— Sarah 1848.
— William 1838.
AVIS Elizabeth 1819.
— George 1804.
— Thomas 1829.

N

BAPTISMS.	MARRIAGES.	BURIALS.

BAPTISMS.

DOWSEN ⎫ Elizabeth 1589.
DOWSYNG ⎭ John 1584.
— Thomas 1593.

EDWARDS Rosa Maria 1866,
ELEY Ann 1821.
— William 1818, 1852.
ELLETT ⎫ Adrie 1600.
ELIOT ⎭ Elizabeth 1595.
— John 1597.
— Rose 1605.
— William 1599.
ELLIS Fred. G. 1830.
— William 1648.
EMMET Ann 1762, 1763, 1764.
— Diana 1729.
— George 1758.
— John 1772.
— Susanna 1767.
— William 1732, 1806.
EVAT Agnes 1665, 1669.
— Ann 1660.
— Elizabeth 1666.
— Frances 1671.
— Francis 1654.
— Henry 1656.
— Margaret 1652.
— Mary 1663.
— Thomas 1657.
EVERARD ⎫ Abraham 1794.
EVERET ⎭ Ann 1707.
— Benjamin 1709.
— Elizabeth 1703, 1738, 1768.
— Francis 1727.
— Frederick 1797.
— George 1859.
— Henry 1724.
— James 1714.
— John 1721, 1722.
— Mabel 1801.
— Mary 1725, 1732.
— Rebecca 1725.
— Robert 1705.
— Rose 1760.
— Samuel 1730.
— Susan 1712.
— Thomas 1721, 1734, 1762,
    1791, 1828.
— William 1728.

MARRIAGES.

EDWARDS Elizabeth 1632.
ELDRED Ann 1716.
— Jone 1588.
ELEY James 1867.
ELLIT ⎫ Audrey 1640.
ELIOT ⎭ Mary 1651.
ELMS Thomas 1712.
EMMET Dinah 1749.
EMINS Barbara 1667.
ERY John 1703.
EVERARD ⎫ Ann 1722.
EVERET ⎭ John 1759.
— Mary 1833.
— Richard 1588, 1702.
— Sarah 1760.
— Thomas 1790.
EWIN Alice 1702.

BURIALS.

EDWARDS Rose Maria 1882.
ELIOT ⎫ Ann 1631.
ELLIT ⎭ Elizabeth, 1655.
— Rose 1667.
— William 1634.
— —— 1647.
ELLIS Hon : Eliza Harriet 1830.
— William 1648.
       See Howard de Walden.
ELY Susan 1871.
— Thomas 1872.
EMMET Ann 1762, 1763, 1795.
— Mary 1802, 1842.
— Susanna 1749.
— William 1730, 1752, 1764,
    1795, 1846.
EVAT Agnes 1665.
— Antony 1646.
— Francis 1665.
— Henry 1656.
— Mary 1664.
EVERARD ⎫ Abraham 1863.
EVERET ⎭ Charlotte 1865.
— Elizabeth 1725, 1771.
— Hannah 1724.
— Henry 1761, 1771.
-- John 1723, 1758, 1773.
— Mary 1733, 1736, 1745,
    1773, 1838.
— Rebecca 1745.
— Richard 1720.
— Robert 1727.
— Rose 1760.
— Sarah 1759.
— Thomas 1722.
— William 1724, 1840.

BAPTISMS.

FENTON Mary 1752.
— William 1754.
FIELD Mary 1677.
— Robert 1673.
FINCH Eliza 1817, 1845.
— Elizabeth 1821.
— John 1812.
— Mary 1843.
— Richard L. 1851.
— Thomas 1814.
FIRMINE Clement 1630.
— Elizabeth 1627, 1655.
— John 1653.
— Mary 1624.
— Susan 1652.
— Thomas 1622.
— Thomasin 1656.
FLACK Vivian Mary 1890.
FORD Elizabeth 1639.
— Margaret 1643.
— Mary 1641, 1645.
FORTUNE Elizabeth 1589.
— Margaret 1594.
— ——— 1592.
FOSTER Augustus J. W. 1780.
FROST Alice 1692.
— Elizabeth 1695.
— Mary 1699.
— Sarah 1761.

GIPPES Mary 1626.
GODFREY Elizabeth 1657.
— Isabel 1663.
— John 1661.
— Sarah 1655.
— Thomas 1668.
GOODALE Robert 1653.
GOODCHILD Alice 1687.
— Arthur 1656, 1686, 1715.
— Edward 1685.
— Elizabeth 1689.
— Frances 1654.
— Francis 1655.
— John 1691.
— Mary 1648, 1677.
— Susan 1652.
— Thomas 1682, 1695.
GOODDAY Eve 1592.
GOSS Ada E. 1852.

MARRIAGES.

FAKES Sophia 1838.
FARRANTS Laura Eliz: 1877.
FARRAR John 1665.
FENTON Samuel 1750.
FILBRIDGE Ann 1620.
FINCHAM Edward 1659.
FIRMIN John 1610.
FISK Robert 1713.
FLATT William 1667.
FORD Mary Ann 1857.
FRANK Mary 1665.
FROST Bridget 1666.
— Francis 1665.
— James 1696.
— Robert 1675, 1760, 1795.
— Rose 1572.
FYNE Barbara 1578.

GALLANT William 1597.
GALT Thomas 1576.
GARDNER Ann 1662.
GASKINNE John 1606.
GARWOOD Charles 1875.
— Martha 1693.
GELLOT Jane 1585.
GENTLEMAN Marian 1738.
GLANVEL Ann 1681.
GOAR Lidea 1684.
GODFREY Elizabeth 1637.
— Ellen 1619.
— John 1684.
GOLDSMITH Susan 1647.
GOODCHILD Arthur 1647, 1676, 1718.
— Mary 1672.
GOODINE Mary 1672.
GOODRICK Ann 1658.

BURIALS.

FENTON Francis 1686.
FIRMIN Susan 1656.
— Thomas 1697.
FORD Elizabeth 1641.
FROGGE William 1609.
FROST Grace 1690.
— John 1799.

GILLOT William 1587.
GIPPS Elizabeth 1604.
GIRR Elizabeth 1820.
GLANVILLE Samuel 1815.
GOLDSMITH Edward 1650.
— Widow 1667.
GOODCHILD Arthur 1686, 1697 1740.
— Frances 1654, 1728.
— Francis 1657.
— Marget 1715.
— Sarah 1711.
— Susan 1675, 1683, 1685.
— Thomas 1685.
GOSS George 1862.
GREEN Ann 1800.
— Jane 1840.
— Maria 1841.
— Sarah 1815.

BAPTISMS .

HERVEY Humphry 1708.
— James A. 1854.
— John 1588, 1616.
— John F. A. 1840.
— Katharine A. G. 1864.
— Katharine P. G. 1848.
— Mary 1589, 1620.
— Mary K. I. 1845.
— Patience M. 1853.
— Robert 1570, 1595.
— Sarah E. H. 1842.
— Susan 1588, 1621.
— Sydenham H. A. 1847.
HEWARD Abigal 1686.
— Dorothy 1651.
— Frances 1654, 1690.
— Mercy 1688.
— Sarah 1685.
HILDERSOM Francis 1587.
— John 1583.
HOLLAX Mary 1689.
HOWE Ann 1832.
— Elizabeth M. 1827.
— Henry 1809.
— James H. 1830.
— Maria 1806.
— Thomas F. 1813.
HOWLETT Dick F. 1872.
— Charlotte E. 1867.
— Melinda 1869.
— William E. 1873.
HUNT Jane 1840.

JAKES Ann 1634. .
JENNISON Eliza 1804.
— Elizabeth 1808.
— Harriet 1809.
— Jane 1812.
— Maria 1805.
— Mary 1814.
JOHNSON Agnes 1575.
— Elias 1634.
— Henry 1631.
— Jone 1583.
— William 1629.

O

MARRIAGES.

HOOD Mary 1698.
HORAX Joshua 1676.
HOUR Rebecca 1814.
HOW Sally 1827.
— Stephen 1744.
HOWARD Martha M. 1740.
HOWLET John 1707.
— Louisa M. A. 1876.
HUGGONS John 1651.
HUNT Jane 1846, 1866.
HURST Isabel 1582.

INSTANCE George 1877.

JAKES Amie 1634.
JOBSON Robert 1632.
JOHNSON Mary 1807.
— Thomas 1659, 1669.
JOLLY Charles 1882.

KEMP Ann 1703.
KING Thomas, 1668.

BURIALS.

HERVEY ⎫ Katharine Isabella
HARVEY ⎭ 1840.
— Lady 1768.
— Lord 1723. 1743, 1796.
— Nicholas 1628.
— Sophia A. E. 1804.
— Sophia Elizabeth 1848.
— Susan 1637.
— Thomas 1694. 1695.
— William 1592, 1642. 1660,
    1663, 1815, 1850.
    See also Bristol, Jermyn,
    Mansel.
HEWARD Abigal 1687.
— Sarah 1685.
HILDER Elizabeth 1737.
HOLDEN Rose 1765.
HOOD Elizabeth 1698.
— Margaret 1691.
HOWARD de WALDEN Lord
    1863.
HOWE Henry 1826.
— James 1848.
— Lucy 1824.
HOWLETT John 1890.
— Melinda 1888.
— Park 1848.
HURST William 1582.

JACKSON Robert 1719.
JERMYN Katherine 1848.
JOHNSON Alice 1583.
— Ann 1579, 1663.
— Robert 1583.
JUNNICLIFF William 1847.

KING Thomas 1583.

BAPTISMS.

LANHAM George E. 1833.
— John 1813.
LARDINER Ann 1576.
— James 1579.
LARNER Thomas 1717.
— William 1714.
LAST Arthur B. 1859.
— Edward H. 1869.
— Rebecca K. 1866.
— Walter F. 1868.
LEONARD | Ann 1816.
LENNARD |David 1814.
— John 1805.
— Phillis 1808.
— Thomas 1806.
LILLY William 1747.
LING Audry 1574.
— Edward 1589.
— Elizabeth 1572, 1708, 1709.
— Frances 1717.
— Gabriel 1618.
— Isabella 1578.
— James 1701, 1711.
— John 1699, 1719.
— Lucy 1703.
— Mary 1576, 1706, 1713, 1722.
— Rebecca 1696.
— Richard 1585.
— Samuel 1706.
— Thomas 1697, 1727.
LOKER Eleanor 1658.
— James 1656.
— John 1648.
— Margaret 1650.
— Mary 1654.
— Robert 1660.
— Susan 1652.

MAIDMENT Henrietta 1845.
MANNING John 1592.
MARTIN John 1615.
— Samuel 1614.
See Cockbill.
MAYE Agnes 1588.
MAYHEW Alfred 1844.
— Elizabeth 1635.
— Emily 1837.
— James 1840.

MARRIAGES.

LANCASTER Sarah 1704.
LANGHAM John 1833.
— Mary 1819.
— Susanna 1826.
LANGLEY John 1572.
— William 1569.
LAST Susan 1674.
LATHAM Robert 1739.
LAWRENCE Frederick 1872.
LEAVER Susan 1723.
LEMING Ann 1669.
LENNARD Thomas 1804.
LIVERMORE Alice 1672.
LIVING John 1718.
LOCKE Randolf 1666.
LOKER Robert 1685.
LYLLY Agnes 1590.
LYNG Ann 1709.
— Audry 1610.
— Edward 1613.
— Elizabeth 1597, 1604.
— Isabel 1601.
— John 1582.
— Robert 1709.
— Thomas 1695.
— William 1569.

MALFALGUERAT Benjamin 1700.
MANNING Ann 1718.
— Isabella 1797.
— Robert 1619.
— Thomas 1698.
MARTIN Frances 1695.
— William 1679.
MASON Benjamin 1807.
— Mary 1702.

BURIALS.

LANGLEY Alice 1593.
— Susan 1570.
— William 1717.
LARDGINE James 1581.
LENNARD Ann 1815, 1816.
— David 1816.
— Mary 1823.
— Mary Ann 1862.
— Thomas 1859.
LING Christian 1711.
— Elizabeth 1708.
— Frances 1745.
— James 1710, 1711.
— John 1717.
— Lucy 1737.
— Mary 1710.
— Samuel 1706.
— Thomas 1731.
— William 1579.
LOKER Eleanor 1658.
— James 1665.
— John 1665, 1675.
— Margaret 1665.
— Mary 1665.
LUNDEN John 1702.

MANNING William 1699.
MANSEL Elizabeth 1727.
MARRAT Isaac 1728.
MASSEY Jane 1851.
MATHEWS Jeffrey 1659.
MAWSON Helen 1883.
MAYHEW Agnes 1588.
— Henry 1573.
— Joseph 1661.
— Thomas 1651(2).

BAPTISMS.

PAIN William B. 1836.
PAMAN George 1574.
— Robert 1567.
PARKER Mary 1601.
PATTLE John 1699.
PAYTEN Ann 1603.
— Elizabeth 1601, 1612.
— Isabel 1605.
— Mary 1609.
— Susanna 1617.
— Thomas 1614.
PEACHEY Ellen E. 1848.
— Frederick 1846.
— Harriet 1840.
— Thomas 1843.
PEPPER Carry 1875.
— Herbert W. 1873.
— Louisa 1883.
PERSON Philippe 1612.
— Richard 1609.
PHIPPS George W. 1748.
PLUM Ann 1825, 1827.
— Hannah 1837.
— Maria 1829.
— Sarah 1832.
POLEY Dorothy 1599.
— Elizabeth 1607.
PRICK ⎰Alice 1782.
PRYKE ⎱Antony T. 1799.
— Benjamin 1785.
— Elizabeth 1739, 1748, 1764.
— Harriet 1793.
— Henry 1787.
— Joseph 1741.
— Lucy 1796.
— Lydia 1774.
— Mary 1746.
— Rose 1811.
— Sarah 1776.
— Sophy 1790.
— Susanna 1743, 1785.

RACE Edgar 1877.
— Elizabeth 1854.
— Frederick 1864.
— Jessie 1860.
— John 1867.
— Jonathan 1862.
RICHARDSON John 1796.

MARRIAGES.

PAIN Walter 1723.
— William 1835.
PALKE Mary 1662.
PAMAN ⎰Elizabeth 1575.
PAMANT ⎱Henry 1624.
— Mary 1660.
— Melysent 1583.
— Sarah 1676.
PARKER John 1604, 1665.
PARMAN John 1658.
PASKE Dorothy 1598.
PAYTON Ann 1624.
— Thomas 1601.
PETTIT Sarah 1722.
— William 1575.
PIKE Ann 1879.
PLUM Maria 1852.
POLE Philip 1578.
POPE James 1835.
POTTER John 1695.
— Mary 1674.
PRATT Joanna 1679.
PRICK Christopher 1674.
— Susanna 1801.
PRIEST Elizabeth 1739.
PRINCE Harriet 1854.

RACE Jessie 1886.
— John 1887.
RATLEY George 1697.
RAVEN Mary 1730.
REDGING Mary 1697.
— Sarah 1640.
REEVE Frances 1665.

BURIALS.

PAIN Sarah 1881.
— William 1702, 1871.
PALEY Cuthbert 1576.
PAMAN Edward 1570.
— John 1570.
PASKE Oliver 1734.
PAYTEN Elizabeth 1601.
PEACHEY Ellen 1849.
PLUMB Ann 1826.
POOL John 1725.
POOLEY Dorothy 1599.
PORTER Keziah 1689.
PREWER Ann 1872.
— John 1888.
PRICK ⎰Benjamin 1844.
PRYKE ⎱Elizabeth 1791.
— Henry 1788.
— Joseph 1782, 1820.
— Mary 1800, 1809.
— Mary Ann 1785.
— Rose 1821.
— Sarah 1818, 1828.
— Susanna 1788.
— Thomas 1758.
— William 1629, 1759.

RACE Edgar 1877.
— Jonathan 1863.
RANSOM Mary 1884.
REINOLDS Ann 1693.
— James 1662.
— Judith 1679.
— Keziah 1694, 1700.

BAPTISMS.

SQUIBBS Maria 1856,
— Patience M. 1860.
— Robert H. 1863.
— Rosetta 1865.
STEEL George 1603.
— Margaret 1599.
— Mary 1606.
— Thomas 1601.
STOCKING | James 1769.
STOCKEN | John 1765.
— Mary 1727, 1733.
— Robert 1764, 1781.
— Rose 1763, 1772.
STUTENILE* Thomas 1605.
SUDBURY Daniel 1634.
— Mary 1631.
— Samuel 1640.
— Susan 1637.
SUMMERS Benjamin 1682, 1724.
— Bridget 1647.
— Elizabeth 1639, 1675.
— John 1650, 1673, 1716.
— Martha 1653.
— Mary 1645.
— Sarah 1639, 1713.
SYER Elizabeth 1802.

TANY Mary 1594.
TILSON John 1772.
TURNER Elizabeth 1670.
— John 1669.
— Margaret 1675.

MARRIAGES.

SPARK Abigall 1701.
— Katharine 1729.
SPARROW Marget 1693.
SPENCELY Thomas 1704.
SPENCER Ann 1679.
— Hugh 1632, 1692.
— Richard 1632.
SPIGHT Christopher 1701.
SPINK Bridget 1606.
SPONELY Edward 1593.
SQUIBBS Maria 1883.
STADE Thomas 1689.
STANDLEY Ann 1597.
STANNARD John 1642.
STEED Elizabeth 1793.
— Mabel 1790.
STEEL Oliver 1597.
STERNE John 1566.
— Mary 1567.
STEWARD Betty 1709.
— John 1709.
— Margaret 1713.
STOCKING Mary 1804.
— Robert 1763.
STONE Edward 1636.
STRATTON Elizabeth 1677.
STURGEON Robert 1709.
SUMMER Elizabeth 1718.
SYER William 1637, 1801.

TALBOT Dine 1621.
THORNE Susan 1676.
THOROGOOD Martha 1763.
THREDDER Andrew 1609.
TILLSON Mary 1772.
TOMSON Matthew 1598.
TRENCH. See Dunlo.
TROUTTEN Thomas 1596.
TUOR Christiana 1723.
TURNER Ann 1659.
— Elizabeth 1661, 1681.
— Frances 1804.
— John 1668.

UMBLETART Richard 1659.
UNDERWOOD Abraham 1682.

BURIALS.

STEED Mabel 1807.
STOCKING Martha 1810.
— Mary 1730, 1749.
— Robert 1765, 1767.
— Rose 1760, 1771, 1772.
STRUTTON Ann 1689.
— George 1696.
— John 1654.
SUDBURY Samuel 1640.
— Susan 1639.
— William 1644.
SUMMERS Benjamin 1745, 1790.
— Bridget 1675.
— Elizabeth 1792.
— John 1673, 1709.
— Sarah 1644, 1714, 1729.

TERRILL Keziah 1659.
TUOR Jane 1758.
TURNER John 1701.
— Mary 1678.
TYLER Elizabeth 1706.

* Probably should be Stutevile.—S. H. A. H.

CPSIA information can be obtained at www.ICGtesting.com
Printed in the USA
LVOW131517270812

296155LV00004B/86/P